THE SECRET INGREDIENT

Sally Bee

THE SECRET INGREDIENT

Sally Bee

Delicious and easy heart-healthy
recipes that might just save your life

STERLING

New York / London
www.sterlingpublishing.com

dedication

I would like to dedicate this book to my family:

To my three precious little food tasters, Tarik, Kazim and Lela.

To Dogan, who has been by my side since my heart attacks to support me but was brave enough to let me go when I needed to get independent again.

To my dad, who supports everything I do and gives the best advice when I can't see the wood for the trees.

And to my mum, Jill, who lost her brave battle with cancer but is still with me in some way every day.

This book is for you, Mum. I so wish you had lived to see it. x

nutritional advice

If you have a particular medical condition that requires a specialist diet, always consult with a medical nutritional expert. I chose to take many different courses in nutrition to help me with my own condition, and developed my recipes accordingly. So although my recipes all promote a sound healthy diet, I am not qualified to give individual advice or suggest recipes for any chronic medical condition. Please also be careful when seeking nutritional advice about a medical condition; always ask your doctor for a recommendation and/or referral to a nutritionist.

STERLING and the distinctive Sterling logo are registered trademarks of Sterling Publishing Co., Inc.

10 9 8 7 6 5 4 3 2 1

Published in the United States by
Sterling Publishing Co., Inc.
387 Park Avenue South, New York, NY 10016

First published in the United Kingdom in 2010 by Collins, an imprint of HarperCollinsPublishers
77-85 Fulham Palace Road
London W6 8JB
www.harpercollins.co.uk

Photography © Kate Whitaker, 2010
Text © Sally Bee, 2010
Layout by www.TheOakStudio.co.uk

Printed in Canada

Sterling ISBN: 978-1-4027-8140-7

For information about custom editions, special sales, premium andcorporate purchases, please contact Sterling Special Sales Departmentat 800-805-5489 or specialsales@sterlingpublishing.com.

contents

my story

My story begins on a lovely sunny, happy day, at a child's birthday party. I was talking to my friends and my husband, Dogan, laughing and watching the children play. One moment, everything was just as it should be, but within one breath, my whole life turned upside down, never to be the same again.

Suddenly I felt extremely poorly. I handed my nine-month-old baby girl to a friend, and ran to the toilet. I had a feeling of impending doom, as if a big black cloud was looming over me, making every breath more meaningful. I understood immediately that something very serious was happening to me and that it was beyond my control. I collapsed on the floor, feeling as if my chest was being crushed and struggling to breathe. I felt sick and hot and sweaty. The pain I was enduring was so much worse than giving birth to any of my three babies.

I managed to get back to my friends, and what followed was chaos. An ambulance was called, and while we waited my kind friends tried in vain to help me – bringing me ice, water and a bag to breathe into. All I wanted at that moment, though, was to stare into my husband's eyes because I needed him to be with me and to understand what I was saying to him. I managed to give him some brief instructions on what to do with the children, but I guess I was telling him something much more than that too.

The ambulance arrived, and the crew checked me over. They managed to calm me down a little and took an ECG (a measurement of the heartbeat). They said there was a slight abnormality, but because of my young age (36) and the fact that I led a healthy lifestyle and there was no family history of heart problems, they were happy to rule out anything serious there and then. Even so, we decided that I should go to the hospital immediately to get properly checked out.

After a few hours spent being looked over, I was eventually let home with some indigestion medicine!

I spent the next couple of days recovering and feeling traumatized by the whole event. I couldn't put my finger on it, but I felt something had changed inside me. A couple of days later, after clearing up the kitchen, the pain hit me again. It felt like a herd of elephants stamping on my chest. Each breath was tight and so painful. If at that moment someone had offered to cut off my right arm so that the pain would go away, I would readily have handed over the knife!

My husband called for an ambulance again, and events at the hospital this time started to unravel, like a really bad soap opera. It started with pure panic. I felt I was not being taken seriously and I was left alone in my cubicle, suffering in agony. I couldn't call anyone to come and help me because the pain literally took my breath away. I thought I might die alone in that cubicle and not be found for hours. Eventually one student nurse looked at my ECG and her jaw dropped. Suddenly, I was no longer alone; the room was buzzing with people all around me. At one point I had three cardiologists looking at my heart trace chart, saying that it was telling them that I was having a heart attack but that they didn't believe it – because of my age, lifestyle, etc.

The next morning, I was told by a cardiologist that my blood tests showed I had suffered a very serious heart attack. I was relieved that I had survived, but felt numb with disbelief. In fact, I got really cross with the doctor for talking such rubbish! I just wanted to go home.

Unfortunately, it was quite a while before I did. Throughout the day, I started to suffer more chest pains. I could feel myself sinking lower and lower and I kept being moved from one bed to another, closer and closer to the Cardiac Care Unit. I needed to be monitored constantly and my heart rhythm was doing some amazing acrobatics. A nurse was sent to take a scan of my heart. I suppose it is down to my natural optimism that I still expected her to say, 'Oh everything's fine ... probably eaten something dodgy!' But her expression was grave. She has since told me that she was shocked – it was the most excessive damage she has ever seen in anyone so young.

I continued to deteriorate and was eventually wheeled into the Coronary Care High Dependency Unit. It had a very different feel about it – all white, very high ceilings, voices echoing. The beds in this unit had very wide spaces between them to accommodate the rescue teams of doctors and nurses. My team came to my rescue at about 5pm. I had sunk so low, the pain in my chest was breaking through the drugs they had given me and I could no longer talk. The only thought in my head was to keep breathing. Breathe in and breathe out, breathe in, breathe out. I figured if I could just keep breathing, I wouldn't die. The doctors and nurses were quickly putting needles and lines into both of my arms and each hand. They were all moving very quickly around me and speaking in hushed voices. I managed to whisper to one of the nurses as she crouched at my bedside and held my hand with great pity in her eyes. She said they were calling my husband to come back – he'd gone home to be with the children for tea. I asked if I was going to die now, and she swallowed hard before saying, 'Not now' – but she gave her colleague a look. She was a lovely gentle nurse but no good at telling lies.

The team managed to stabilize me enough to move me to another hospital, where, they said, I would get fixed up. They had arranged for me to have an angiogram, expecting to find a blockage somewhere in my heart that was causing the problem.

An angiogram involves inserting a tube, via a vein in your groin, into the heart. Dye is pumped through the tube and an x-ray shows the blood and oxygen flow and any blockage. If there is a blockage, it can often be cleared by fitting a stent or by performing a bypass.

At this point, I was passing in and out of consciousness. I was aware that I was just hanging on, and wasn't at all sure how much longer I would manage. We arrived at the new hospital, and the surgeon, who had been dragged out of bed, told me all the risks associated with an angiogram and the mortality rate. Even in my perilous state, I could do the maths – and thought there were things I'd much rather have been doing.

The Cath Lab, where they were going to perform the procedure, was very cold and I had to lie on an even colder table to have the angiogram. By this point I was relatively relaxed, partly due to the drugs I had been given but also partly because of what was happening to my body. I was starting to shut down. I felt myself let go a couple of times and it frightened me ... but it was not unpleasant. It would have been very easy just to drift off. I knew my situation was very bad but the thing that surprised me was how calm I was by then.

The surgeon started his procedure, putting a small incision in my groin. I felt the blood trickle over my leg. He then fed the line up into my heart to pump the dye in and x-ray the results. I felt very close to the edge, but I was still quietly determined just to keep breathing. Yet I almost gave up when I heard the surgeon start to swear under his breath. I looked at his face and saw an expression of shock and disbelief and then panic and then nothing. It was when he started to swear that I think I began to understand just how dire my situation was.

Even so, I wasn't prepared for what happened next. The surgeon took off his gloves, then left the room with his shoulders drooped. The nurses and assistants followed quietly as if embarrassed – I was all alone. Everyone really had gone. Upped and left. Gone. I was alone. Completely and utterly alone in this dreadful room on this cold table. I thought for a moment that I was dead and this was what it was like.

I stopped forcing my breath and let my natural breath take over. Each breath was so shallow and light but it was all I could hear in the room. I couldn't fill my lungs. Was I still alive? I could drift off really easily and when I did the pain in my chest went away. I did it a couple of times to see what it was like. It was fine. Just fine. I would then pull myself back and the hurting returned, but it had turned into a 'good' pain because it proved that I was still alive. I really needed that confirmation. And I really needed to feel the pain.

After what seemed like a couple of hours, but which was probably only a couple of minutes, Dogan, my husband, walked into the room. He was sobbing. He said that he loved me. The doctors had told him that I had suffered another massive heart attack; that my heart had sustained a shocking amount of damage, which could not be repaired; and that I was going to die. So as he walked into the lab, he was coming to say goodbye.

I would love to be able to write that I told him how much I loved him and we held each other tight. That didn't happen. Since I had just discovered that I was still alive, and I'd allowed myself to think for a second about my little ones at home, I was filled with an all-consuming need and desire and passion not to let myself die. I can't put into words how strong this feeling was. It was this surge of emotion that literally saved my life. It must have been all about the people that I love. It was instinctive and I decided there and then that I would never, ever give up breathing.

I had so much to live for.

What had actually happened to my heart was something so rare that none of the cardiologists that I saw subsequently had ever encountered it before. In fact, it was the reason the surgeon had become so defeated and left me in the lab. My main left artery, the one inside the heart that feeds the heart muscle blood and oxygen, had literally unravelled and fallen apart. The condition is called 'spontaneous coronary artery dissection', and is usually diagnosed post-mortem. My artery just simply fell apart, which meant that the blood coming into the heart, instead of being pumped straight out to feed my body, was actually just leaking away. My heart was literally bleeding and being starved of the blood and oxygen that it needed to function, and my body and vital organs were also being deprived. I had just enough output, or blood trickling through, to keep me alive. Just.

At this point, I was wired up to monitors and machines and felt overwhelmed and in a complete state of shock. Nobody can really explain why I survived that night. According to all the medical books, I shouldn't have. My condition is incredibly rare, with only 200 or so recorded cases worldwide and about 30 survivors – ever! However, I was also fit, a healthy eater and a non-smoker, so this all worked in my favour. I am also a great believer in fate, and with three babies at home I had the most precious of reasons to keep breathing.

I could tell that the doctors were struggling the next day to say something positive to me. But they couldn't. They believed that although I had survived the heart attacks, my chances of pulling through the next 24 hours were very slim. They were kind and gentle but, in this instance, they couldn't perform miracles.

eating for health

Well, as you have probably gathered, having survived the un-survivable, my future health became so very important to me. I realized that I was the only person who could control how long I was to be around. Food and exercise became my saviour – and this book is my eating plan.

Here, you will find the recipes I devised when my prognosis was poor and I knew I had to take control of everything I ate in order to give myself the best possible chance of survival. At the same time I had three hungry cherubs at home and I was determined that they should grow up with a great relationship with food, as I had. I certainly didn't want them to grow up thinking that a diet of mung beans and spinach was normal! So, scattered through my recipes you will find some ingredients often considered 'unhealthy'. I'd like to take the opportunity to address each of these so that you fully understand what the facts are.

The first point to make is that 'good food' and 'bad food' is an old message steeped in myth and half-truth. I believe that many people have picked up unhelpful pieces of advice that they now hang on to, but actually these so-called 'facts' are making it far more difficult for them to enjoy a healthy diet for life. I know that the key to eating well is balancing nourishment with enjoyment; moderation is essential and it is possible to eat for health and taste in equal measure. I hope that after reading my book you'll find it very easy to make good food choices and at the same time enjoy your food as you deserve to.

So, you'll see that some delicious recipes that contain **red meat**. It is true that chicken and fish would usually be the preferred option; however, red meat is a valuable source of iron and zinc and eaten in small quantities is good for you. Be sure to buy top-quality lean meat and always cut off all visible fat. All of my dishes that contain red meat also have a high vegetable content and so are perfectly balanced to give your body the nutrients it needs.

Some recipes contain a little **butter** or **cheese**. They are a good source of calcium, however, and the quantities used are very small. What's more the dishes are designed to feed at least four people and so do not contain enough dairy to be detrimental to your health when eaten in moderation.

Keep a close watch on which dishes are marked **'everyday'** and which are marked **'treat'**. I have done this to guide you. An 'everyday' dish speaks for itself, but try to limit the 'treats' to once a week or once every two weeks to be on the fun side of safe!

Potatoes get a bad press – possibly because we often think of them loaded with fat as chips and crisps. However, in their natural form they are fat free, high in

fibre and a good source of vitamin C. They are also affordable, keep well and are incredibly versatile. I use potatoes all the time, such as when I need to bulk out a meal if we have unexpected guests.

I suspect that some of you will have been put off potatoes because of the recent fashion for carbohydrate-free diets. However, please understand that your body needs a little carbohydrate every day and it's much better to get it from a high-fibre food like a potato than a low-fibre starchy food like bread or pasta.

Eggs also have an unfairly bad reputation. They contain cholesterol, and so it is often thought that people who have high blood cholesterol should not eat eggs. Actually, the cholesterol in an egg is not absorbed into the blood stream. Each yolk contains around 5g of fat (about 8 per cent of the daily amount we should have), of which only 1.5g is saturated (i.e. bad for you). Although they should not be eaten every day, they are a good source of protein and contain more than a dozen vitamins and minerals, including iron, zinc, phosphorus, folate, riboflavin, vitamins A, D, E and B12. So you can see that from a nourishment point of view an egg packs quite a punch! I'd call that healthy eating, wouldn't you?

I have included some of my favourite family recipes, such as lasagne, shepherd's pie and even egg and chips (see pages 95, 99 and 41)! Take a closer look and you'll see that even these recipes contain only a little olive oil and are packed with nutrients from the high vegetable content. For most people, nutrition is an art and not a science. We all wish to eat well and be healthy and my recipes will help you achieve just that. I want you and your family to enjoy a healthy diet as much as my family and I do.

Enjoy!

p.s. The oven temperatures in this book are for a conventional oven. If you are using a fan oven, follow the manufacturer's instructions.

soups & starters

carrot and butternut squash soup

everyday

This soup is so quick and easy to make and is wonderfully good for you. It will keep for up to a week in the refrigerator.

serves 4

1 red onion, peeled and finely chopped

2 garlic cloves, peeled and finely chopped

2 tbsp olive oil

4 large carrots, peeled

1 medium butternut squash, peeled and deseeded

freshly ground black pepper

850ml/1½ pints/3¾ cups chicken or vegetable stock

2–3 fresh thyme sprigs, leaves picked

handful of chopped fresh parsley or coriander (cilantro)

1 Sweat the onion and garlic in the olive oil over a medium heat in a large, lidded pan for about 7 minutes, or until soft.

2 Chop the carrots and butternut squash into 1.5cm/⅝in cubes and add to the pan. Season with black pepper and cook for another 10 minutes, or until the vegetables start to soften.

3 Pour in the stock, add the thyme leaves and parsley or coriander (cilantro) and bring to the boil. Now turn down the heat a little, cover and simmer for about 30 minutes.

4 Finally, use a hand blender or liquidizer to purée the soup. Reheat and serve.

courgette and pea soup

everyday

An easy-to-make soup that is packed with beta-carotene, vitamin C and folate. Tastes good too!

1 Heat the olive oil in a medium-sized saucepan over a moderate heat. Add the courgettes (zucchini) and onion and sauté for about 10 minutes, or until the vegetables start to soften.

2 Pour in the stock, then bring to the boil, lower the heat and simmer, covered, for 15 minutes.

3 Add the peas to the soup and simmer for a further 5 minutes.

4 Blend the soup in a liquidizer or blender and stir in the basil.

5 Reheat, season to taste with black pepper and serve immediately.

serves 6.

dash of olive oil

4 small courgettes (zucchini), chopped into small pieces

1 small onion, peeled and sliced

900ml/1½ pints/3½ cups chicken stock

225g/8oz/2 cups fresh or frozen peas

25g/1oz fresh basil, torn

freshly ground black pepper

exercise – the secret ingredient

I know we'd all like to take a magic pill that will make us healthier and help us to lose weight. Wouldn't it be wonderful if that pill could also reverse our heart disease, stop us from getting cancer, help us look younger, and actually make our whole lives happier, easier and longer?

Well, there is something that will do all of the above, but it is not in the form of a tablet. You don't even need to get it on prescription. And it is not so secret after all, although many people seem to have problems realizing how easy it is to do and how fast the benefits will come.

The Secret Ingredient is simply increased physical activity. There's nothing like it, and there's nothing that will replace it!

I'm not necessarily talking about joining a gym or getting into pink and purple Lycra, leg warmers and 'feeling the burn', but I do practise what I preach and I call it 'active living'.

When I first came out of hospital after my heart attacks, all I could manage were a few steps to and from my front gate. I couldn't manage the short walk to pick my son up from school like the other mums, so I had to be inventive to keep up appearances. I would spend all day getting ready. I'd have a shower – then sleep for an hour. Dry my hair – exhausting work – then sleep for two hours. Add a bit of lippy – another nap and it'd be time to go.

I'd get a lift around the corner to the school and would then settle myself on the school bench before all the parents arrived, and when they did, I would smile and wave as if everything were completely normal. I did catch a few looks, as if to say, 'I thought she was meant to be ill; she looks OK to me!' I would then manage to stand up to greet my little man as he ran out of school, and give him the big hug that he'd been waiting for. Luckily, he was happy to be walked home by a friend; he didn't seem too bothered that I didn't actually walk him home, only that I was there to see him when he first came out of the school door. I would then sit back down on my 'life-saving' bench and wait for all the other parents to go before I'd catch my lift back home again.

baby step by baby step

Each time I did this little journey, I was left completely exhausted. Add to this challenge that I also had a nine-month-old baby girl and a very active two-year-old at home. For obvious reasons, I had to have a full-time nanny for a while to do all the physical stuff, but I even found talking to my little ones incredibly tiring. However, because I had started to push myself, baby step by baby step, I soon realized that I was getting stronger. I knew my heart was very damaged, and none of the doctors could give me a positive prognosis for survival at this stage. Thankfully, I started to tune in to my body and *listen* to what it was telling me. When I felt strong enough, I started to walk for maybe three or four minutes. Other days, I could manage only one or two. Little by little, step by step, I built my strength to the level that I'm at now.

Would you be surprised to hear that I now exercise *every* day? I swim, I walk, I cycle with the kids. I don't do anything dramatic, I keep my heart rate nice and steady. I allow myself to get gently out of breath, never gasping, and I still listen to my body. When it tells me it's time to stop and rest, I do just that.

The good news is that it works. My cardiologists are amazed at my recovery. They cannot believe the levels of fitness that I have achieved and the way my heart is responding. I am so happy that I have taken control of my 'active living', and it is having such a positive effect on my health that I wouldn't want to live my life any other way.

So back to the Secret Ingredient – why don't you try a bit of active living yourself? Enjoy your food, eat for health by following some of my recipes, then go for a walk! Make a resolution to begin today. Start by just taking a walk around the block. Then build it up slowly, listening to your body. Walk as though you are late for an appointment. When you're on the telephone, walk around instead of sitting still. Go for a wander in the park at lunchtime. Do your grocery shopping in half the time it usually takes you. Before you know it, you will start to lose a little weight, you'll start to feel a bit more energetic, and you'll probably want to try some other activities: cycling, swimming, gardening, dancing, or anything else you enjoy that will get your heart rate up.

Promise yourself you'll live actively for three months. If you can honestly say after that trial period that you don't feel 100 per cent better, then quit. But you will feel better, and you won't quit.

The Secret Ingredient. Try it, you'll like it – I promise!

easy hummus

everyday

Great as a starter with some toasted wholemeal (whole-wheat) pitta bread or vegetable sticks.

serves 4

2 small garlic cloves, peeled and roughly chopped

1 mild red chilli, deseeded and roughly chopped

400g/14oz can chickpeas, drained and rinsed

4 tbsp extra-virgin olive oil

handful fresh flat-leaf parsley or coriander (cilantro), roughly chopped

juice of ½ lemon

freshly ground black pepper

1 Put the garlic, chilli, chickpeas and 1-2 tablespoons olive oil in a food processor and whiz until completely smooth – this may take several minutes. Add the herbs and a squeeze of lemon juice and whiz again until well blended. Taste and add more lemon juice and olive oil, as needed, plus some black pepper.

2 Spoon into a serving bowl and drizzle over a little more oil, then cover and chill in the fridge until ready to serve.

sardine and olive tapenade
everyday

For a delicious starter, load this tasty tapenade onto small slices of wholemeal (whole-wheat) toast for a flavour explosion!

1 Put all the ingredients into a food processor, or use a hand blender and a large bowl. Whiz until you have a coarse paste.

2 Taste to check the balance of flavours and add a little extra lemon juice if needed.

3 Serve on small pieces of toasted wholemeal bread.

serves 6

150g/5½oz/scant 1 cup pitted black olives

3 sardine fillets (canned, in tomato sauce)

3 tbsp capers (in brine, rinsed and drained)

2 tsp dried rosemary

1 heaped tsp fennel seeds

zest of 1 lemon

squeeze of fresh lemon juice

2 tbsp extra-virgin olive oil

freshly ground black pepper

the five 'f's

I'm going to share with you my most precious tool for maintaining good health and happiness: the five 'F's. **Family. Food. Fitness. Finance. Future.** Pay attention to these and your life will change! It's just a way of altering your thinking – of paying attention to the simple but important things in life, and it works for me.

Family is the most important element, I would imagine, in everyone's life. And the older you get, the more precious your family becomes, especially if along the way you have lost a close family member. We can all show our family how much we care by feeding them well and by nourishing them with healthy **food**. As a mother, I know that my happiest moments in the day are when my children eat a lovely meal that I've cooked for them and they leave the table glowing, eyes sparkling and full of energy! So, by caring for a family through food, you are enabling **fitness**. Kids have good energy to play, adults have good energy to work, play sports and make the most of life. When we have good fitness, we also have the energy to take care of our **finances**. We are more efficient, we can work until the job gets done and be satisfied we have achieved our best, financially. And this in turn leads to a better **future** – physically, emotionally and financially.

the rainbow

When you are planning your 'five a day', try to think about a rainbow. The more colours you can incorporate into your diet, the healthier you'll be.

   If you are not aware of the need to eat five fruit and vegetable portions, it's easy to eat only two or three portions day. The most important thing is to count and rotate your foods throughout the week. Eating a rainbow of colours is the best way to ensure that you are getting your full quota of nutrients. It's the phytochemicals that give fruit their colour, so if you eat lots of different-coloured fruit and vegetables, you get a whole range of benefits.

RED: tomatoes and watermelon contain the essential nutrient lycopene.

ORANGE: mangoes and oranges contain plenty of vitamin C, and carrots and sweet potatoes are rich in beta-carotene.

YELLOW: sweetcorn (corn), pineapples and yellow (bell) peppers contain lutein (a form of antioxidant), and bananas provide potassium, which helps to prevent heart rhythm irregularities.

GREEN: broccoli, cabbage, Brussels sprouts and watercress contain folic acid, which helps to maintain healthy arteries.

BLUE: blueberries, blackberries and prunes are full of healthy vitamins and anthocyanin, which helps circulation.

INDIGO AND VIOLET: beetroot (beet), aubergines (eggplants), plums and red cabbage all contain powerful antioxidants.

Research shows that people who have a diet high in antioxidants tend to have a lower risk of heart disease and cancer compared to people whose diets lack these vital nutrients.

salads, sides & vegetarian

chargrilled vegetable salad
everyday

Ideally you'll need a grill pan for this dish, or a George Foreman-style grill.

serves 4

olive oil, to brush the griddle pan

1 large aubergine (eggplant), sliced lengthways

2 large courgettes (zucchini), sliced lengthways

8 spring onions (scallions), blanched in boiling water for 2 minutes

1 red and 1 yellow (bell) pepper, roasted, skinned, deseeded and cut into quarters

12 asparagus spears

for the grilled vegetable marinade:

1 shallot, peeled and diced

1 red chilli, deseeded and finely diced

2 garlic cloves, peeled and diced

8 basil leaves, torn

2 tbsp extra-virgin olive oil

1 tbsp sherry vinegar

1 Set a non-stick ridged griddle pan over a high heat and brush lightly with olive oil.

2 Cook all the vegetables for 2–3 minutes on each side until nicely chargrilled (charbroiled), then remove from the heat.

3 In a large bowl, combine all the marinade ingredients and add the cooked vegetables, gently stirring and coating them in the marinade. Leave, covered, in the fridge to marinate thoroughly – overnight if possible – and serve the next day at room temperature. Don't worry if making this is a last-minute decision and you don't have time to marinate overnight. Just let the flavours infuse for as long as you can.

crunchy coleslaw

everyday

This makes a great accompaniment to any dish. But I love it on its own, sneaking a nibble as I'm passing the refrigerator!

1 Wash the cabbage, carrots and apple.

2 Shred the cabbage and apple and grate the carrots. Don't even think about getting a machine to do this for you – it's great exercise for those arms! Put into a colourful bowl, then add all the other ingredients. Mix up well, having a little taste as you go.

3 Garnish with the chopped chervil or parsley and serve.

My recipes are very low salt. If you're missing salt, try a squeeze of lemon instead for that extra zing.

serves 10

½ small white cabbage

2 carrots

1 small green apple

juice of ½ lemon

1 tbsp extra-virgin olive oil

150g/5½oz/⅔ cup natural low-fat yogurt

freshly ground black pepper

chopped fresh chervil or flat-leaf parsley, to garnish

herbed leaf salad

everyday

A wooden bowl is recommended for this dish – for a unique way to flavour the salad.

serves 4–6

1 garlic clove, peeled

4 tbsp mixed fresh herbs (chervil, tarragon, dill, basil, marjoram, flat-leaf parsley, mint, chives, sorrel)

350g/12oz mixed salad leaves, washed, dried and torn (curly endive, baby spinach, rocket/arugula, radicchio, chicory, watercress, treviso, oak leaf, dandelion, nasturtium)

freshly ground black pepper

to serve (optional):

wholemeal (whole-grain) croutons

toasted pine nuts

shavings of Parmesan

for the dressing:

2 tbsp extra-virgin olive oil

2 tbsp balsamic vinegar

juice of 1 lemon

1 tsp wholegrain mustard

½ tsp muscovado sugar

1 Rub a wooden salad bowl with the raw garlic. Combine the herbs and the salad leaves and mix thoroughly. Season with black pepper.

2 For the dressing, put the olive oil, balsamic vinegar, lemon juice, mustard and sugar into a cup or small bowl and whisk together with a fork quite vigorously.

3 Dress the leaves, but don't drown them. Serve immediately – once dressed, try not to let the salad sit around for too long, or the leaves will go soggy. If you like, scatter over some wholemeal (whole-grain) croutons, toasted pine nuts or flakes (slivers) of Parmesan.

prawn, avocado and pecan herb salad

everyday

You know, salads don't have to be boring. This dish is full of flavour! You can serve it as a main meal or smaller portions for a healthy starter. If you don't like prawns, you can substitute with chicken; anything goes, really. Be adventurous with your salads and make this a regular, everyday dish.

Prawns give great texture and flavour to this recipe, but they do contain cholesterol, so I have allowed only four prawns per serving. If you want to make it more substantial, you can add extra protein: such as tuna, chicken or turkey.

1 Heat the olive oil in a large frying pan over a medium heat. Add the chopped salad onions, crushed garlic, soy sauce, black pepper and raw prawns. Sauté until the prawns have turned pink all the way through.

2 Arrange the salad leaves, watercress, avocado and tomatoes in a big dish, then pour over the prawns and other cooked ingredients. Squeeze over the lemon juice, sprinkle with torn basil and pecan nuts and serve.

serves 2

drizzle of olive oil

2 salad onions or spring onions (scallions), peeled and finely chopped

1 garlic clove, peeled and crushed

1 tbsp soy sauce

freshly ground black pepper

8 uncooked king prawns (jumbo shrimp)

mixed salad leaves

watercress

1 ripe avocado

2 tomatoes, sliced

juice of 1 lemon

handful of fresh basil, torn

handful of shelled pecan nuts

the 'staying alive as long as possible' plan

I enjoy giving talks to different heart rehab groups and medical conferences around the country. I love hearing people's amazing stories and I love to learn different tips to make life a little easier after surviving a trauma. Something that people in my heart groups seem to really struggle with when recovering from any incident is learning how to rest properly. For some reason, we seem to feel guilty when we need to rest and see it as some sort of failure.

I have always been a busy Bee! So having rest forced upon me after my heart attacks was difficult to accept. For a long time I tried to fight it, until one day I had one of those 'light bulb' moments when everything suddenly made perfect sense and I no longer viewed resting in a negative way.

I realized that the problem with my heart was playing with my head. I was frightened that I was going to die because my heart would simply stop working. So whenever I got tired and needed to rest, I started to panic, thinking I was going to die any second. Looking back, I can see how ridiculous this mindset was, but it made perfect sense to me at the time.

One day, I had a visit from my friend Mark (who thinks he is the local answer to David Beckham!). He'd been playing five-a-side football and had suffered a yukky-looking injury to his thigh. Anyway, he popped in, all sweat and drama, and immediately put his damaged leg up on my sofa to rest it and announced that he wouldn't be able to work for at least a week with this terrible injury … It suddenly dawned on me that his condition wasn't going to play with his head in the way mine did because his was his leg – not a vital organ. Further, the fact that this was a common injury made it easier for him to understand how important it was to let his thigh muscle rest and heal and regain its strength if he was ever going to reach the dizzy heights of five-a-side captain again! Well, if Mark could do that for his leg, why couldn't I view my heart in the same light? My heart had suffered a trauma in the same way as Mark's thigh. His leg got a chance to rest properly, yet my heart was always working hard, pumping away. Mark accepted that rest was important, yet I was fighting it all the way. It was time to get real.

Here's my new philosophy on rest: I now try to do everything 100 per cent. When I am busy, I am busy 100 per cent. When I need to rest, I rest 100 per cent. There is no point in taking a half-hearted rest (as it were); you may as well not bother!

I have a three-point 'staying alive as long as possible' plan:

- **I eat well** to nourish my body
- **I exercise** and move about as quickly as possible
- **I embrace my rest** – it's just as important as the other points and allows my body to fix and recover, and gives me support for upcoming excitement and adventure!

Mark, you'll be glad to know, is still playing footie – albeit with a limp …

italian-style courgettes

everyday

Classic, Italian-style, full of natural flavour. I was given this recipe about 20 years ago and have cooked it again and again ... and again.

1 Heat the oil in a large frying pan and fry the onion and garlic over a moderate heat for 5-6 minutes, or until the onion has softened and is beginning to brown.

2 Add the courgette (zucchini) slices and fry for about 4 minutes, or until they just begin to be flecked with brown on both sides. Stir frequently.

3 Stir in the stock, fresh oregano and black pepper, and simmer gently for about 8-10 minutes, or until the liquid has almost evaporated. Spoon the courgettes into a serving dish, sprinkle with chopped parsley and serve.

These courgettes make a quick, healthy snack.

serves 4

1 tbsp olive oil

1 large onion, peeled and chopped

1 garlic clove, peeled and crushed

4–5 medium courgettes (zucchini), sliced

150ml/5fl oz/ ⅔ cup hot home-made chicken or vegetable stock

½ tsp chopped fresh oregano

freshly ground black pepper

chopped fresh flat-leaf parsley, to garnish

baked crusty fennel

everyday

The refreshing, delicate aniseed flavour of the fennel in the dish is complemented by the crispy crust.

serves 4

3 fennel bulbs, cut lengthways into quarters

2 tbsp olive oil

1 garlic clove, peeled and chopped

55g/2oz/1 cup day-old wholemeal (whole-wheat) breadcrumbs

2 tbsp chopped fresh flat-leaf parsley

freshly ground black pepper

1 Preheat the oven to 190°C/375°F/Gas mark 5.

2 Cook the fennel in a large saucepan of boiling water for 10 minutes.

3 Drain the fennel and place in a large ovenproof baking dish or baking tray, then brush with half of the olive oil.

4 In a small bowl, mix together the garlic, breadcrumbs and parsley, then stir in the rest of the olive oil. Sprinkle the mixture evenly over the fennel, then season well with black pepper.

5 Bake the fennel for about 30 minutes, or until it is tender and the breadcrumb topping is crisp and golden brown. Serve the baked fennel hot, as an accompaniment to any meat or fish dish.

roasted garlic tomatoes

everyday

This is one of my favourite things! I love the rich flavour. It doesn't surprise me that cooked tomatoes are incredibly beneficial to the heart. Something that tastes this good has got to be good for the heart. I'm in love!

serves 2-3

2 whole garlic bulbs

6 large beef (beefsteak) tomatoes or 12 smaller tomatoes (organic of course)

2 garlic cloves

1 tbsp olive oil

1 tsp mixed dried herbs

good sprinkling of freshly ground black pepper

sprinkling of celery salt

2 tsp sugar

torn fresh basil

1 Preheat the oven to 200ºC/400ºF/Gas mark 6.

2 Slice the very top off the whole garlic bulbs to expose the tops of the cloves and place in the centre of a roasting tray.

3 Wash the tomatoes and cut into halves.

4 Peel and crush the garlic cloves (or chop them very finely).

5 Put the oil, garlic and dried herbs into a large bowl.

6 Add the tomato halves and stir until well coated with the oil and flavourings. Then place into the roasting tin and sprinkle with black pepper, celery salt and sugar. Place in the oven for 40-50 minutes, or until the tomatoes are golden on top and nicely caramelized.

7 Sprinkle over the fresh basil. To serve, squeeze the soft, roasted garlic out of its skin and serve with the tomatoes.

Keep these in the fridge for 2-3 days and add to other dishes, such as pasta and salads.

braised baby leeks in red wine with aromatics

*everyday**

You can either serve these on their own, or as an accompaniment (they go wonderfully with Spicy Couscous, see page 38). You may prefer to leave them to cool. If you chill them, bring them back to room temperature before serving. Sprinkle over the chopped herbs just before serving.

1 If using baby leeks, simply trim the ends, but leave them whole. Cut thick leeks into 5-7.5cm/2-3in lengths.

2 Place the coriander seeds and cinnamon in a pan wide enough to take all the leeks in a single layer. Dry-fry over a medium heat for 2-3 minutes, or until the spices give off a fragrant aroma, then stir in the olive oil, bay leaves, orange rind, fresh or dried oregano, sugar, wine and balsamic or sherry vinegar. Bring to the boil, then simmer for 5 minutes. (The alcohol will burn off.)

3 Add the leeks to the pan. Bring back to the boil, reduce the heat and cover the pan. Cook the leeks gently for 5 minutes. Uncover and simmer gently for another 5-8 minutes, or until the leeks are just tender when tested with the tip of a sharp knife.

4 Use a slotted spoon to transfer the leeks to a warmed serving dish. Boil the pan juices rapidly until reduced to about 5-6 tablespoons.

5 Add black pepper to taste and pour the liquid over the leeks.

serves 4

12 baby leeks or 6 thick leeks

1 tbsp coriander seeds, lightly crushed

5cm/2in piece of cinnamon stick

2 tbsp extra-virgin olive oil

3 fresh bay leaves

2 strips of pared orange rind

5-6 fresh or dried oregano sprigs

1 tsp sugar

1 large glass fruity red wine (300ml/10fl oz/1¼ cups)

2 tsp balsamic or sherry vinegar

freshly ground black pepper

* feel free to swap the red wine for some red grape juice

sicilian tomatoes

everyday

Firm round beef (beefsteak) tomatoes are perfect for this dish, to serve as a tasty snack or a meal accompaniment. The taste of the Mediterranean is as wonderful as ever. Feel free to swap the chicken for some fresh tuna steak or tinned tuna.

1 Preheat the oven to 180°C/350°F/Gas mark 4.

2 Slice the top off each tomato and carefully scoop out the pulp and seeds to make a container. Chop the tops and pulp and reserve for later.

3 In a large frying pan, heat the olive oil over a medium heat. Add the onion, garlic and pine nuts and cook for about 7 minutes.

4 Stir in the breadcrumbs and chicken. Cook for a further couple of minutes.

5 Remove from the heat and stir in the oregano or marjoram, capers, olives and some black pepper. Now add the tomato pulp and the dash of Tabasco. Give it all a good stir.

6 Spoon the mixture back into the tomato skins and add a thin slice of mozzarella on top of each tomato.

7 Place on a baking tray and cook for 30 minutes, or until tender and the cheese has turned golden. Serve hot or cold.

serves 4–6

6 beef (beefsteak) tomatoes

2 tbsp olive oil

1 medium onion, peeled and very finely chopped

1 garlic clove, peeled and crushed

15g/½oz/scant 2 tbsp pine nuts

55g/2oz/1 cup wholemeal (whole-wheat) breadcrumbs

175g/6oz cooked chicken, finely chopped

1 tbsp fresh chopped oregano or marjoram

2 tsp capers, chopped

4 black olives, pitted and chopped

freshly ground black pepper

dash of Tabasco sauce

25g/1oz low-fat mozzarella cheese

glazed sweet potatoes
with ginger

everyday*

Absolutely, mouthwateringly delicious. Makes a lovely accompaniment to a light salad or any chicken dish.

Although this recipe contains a little butter, it's a very small amount and adds such a lovely flavour that I think in this instance it's well worth it!

serves 4

900g/2lb sweet potatoes

55g/2oz/½ stick unsalted butter

3 tbsp olive oil

2 garlic cloves, peeled and crushed

2 pieces stem ginger (preserved ginger), finely chopped

2 tsp ground allspice

1 tbsp syrup from the jar of stem ginger (preserved ginger)

cayenne pepper, to taste

2 tsp chopped fresh thyme, plus a few sprigs to garnish

1 Peel the sweet potatoes and cut into 1cm/½in cubes.

2 Melt the butter with the oil in a large frying pan. Add the sweet potato cubes and fry on a medium heat, stirring frequently, for about 10 minutes, or until they are just soft.

3 Stir in the garlic, ginger and ground allspice. Cook, stirring occasionally, for 5 minutes more. Stir in the ginger syrup, a generous pinch of cayenne pepper and the chopped thyme. Stir for 1-2 minutes more, then serve in warmed bowls scattered with fresh thyme sprigs.

* this qualifies as everyday because you have only a small amount as an accompaniment

baked sweet potatoes

everyday

I *love* baked sweet potatoes especially if I'm really starving. I feel I can eat a great big plateful and know that I am filling myself up with energy and goodness.

Because sweet potatoes are much more moist than ordinary potatoes, you will not need to add any butter, but you can be as inventive as you like with fillings.

1 Preheat the oven to 220ºC/425ºF/Gas mark 7.

2 Scrub the sweet potatoes and place on a baking sheet after giving them a couple of stabs with a sharp knife (they have a tendency to leak a bit during cooking).

3 Cook the potatoes for 50 minutes, or until tender. Remove from the oven and prick with a fork to let the steam out.

4 Cut a 4cm/1½in cross in the centre of each potato. Hold each potato and press upwards until the filling 'bursts' up through the cuts.

5 Top with your chosen filling and enjoy!

serves 4

4 medium sweet potatoes, even in size

for the fillings:

sprinkling of paprika
or

heated sweetcorn (corn)
or

sprinkling of low-fat mature hard grated cheese
or

low-salt baked beans
or

canned tuna fish (in brine) drained and mixed with lemon juice and black pepper

roast potatoes à la patrick

everyday/treat*

One of my neighbours, Patrick, taught me how to make these scrumptious yet very easy roast potatoes. This recipe does use a small amount of salt, which I usually avoid, but as long as you've cut down on all processed food with added salt, a tiny bit with your fresh food occasionally will do you no harm (see page 106). This recipe isn't just limited to potatoes. You can roast carrots and parsnips in the same way, or all jumbled in together – gorgeous!

serves 4–6

900g/2lb floury (mealy) potatoes

4 tbsp extra-virgin olive oil

1 tsp celery salt

2 tsp onion powder

2 tsp garlic powder

2–3 fresh rosemary sprigs

1 Preheat the oven to 200°C/400°F/Gas mark 6.

2 Peel, halve and quarter the potatoes. There is no need to parboil the potatoes. Place in a roasting tray (sheet) and drizzle with the olive oil so that the potatoes are glistening all over but not drenched!

3 Next, sprinkle with the celery salt, onion powder and garlic powder. Make sure that all potatoes have a light dusting of these flavours. Add the sprigs of fresh rosemary and put into the oven, turning occasionally, for about 1 hour.

4 When finished, the potatoes should be nicely browned.

Big tip: Use a non-stick baking liner that you cut to fit your roasting tray – it stops anything and everything from sticking and means you don't need to grease the tin.

*everyday – small portion / treat – larger portion

buffalo-style cheese on toast

everyday

Cheese on toast is an old favourite, but most cheese has a high saturated fat content. By using a low-fat mozzarella cheese you cut the fat content and can still enjoy a quick and delicious snack.

1 Toast the bread on both sides under the grill (broiler).

2 Don't butter the toast. Instead, spread the wholegrain mustard onto the slice.

3 Place the slices of tomato and mozzarella on top.

4 Finally add a slurp of Worcestershire sauce and some black pepper.

5 Pop back under the grill for a couple of minutes, watching all the time until the cheese starts to bubble.

serves 1

1 slice wholemeal (whole-wheat) brown bread

½ teaspoon wholegrain mustard

3 slices tomato

3 slices of low-fat mozzarella cut from a mozzarella ball

slurp of Worcestershire sauce

freshly ground black pepper

being healthy is a good thing

I speak to lots of groups of people around the country about my story and offer heart-healthy advice. Many of the people I talk to have just suffered a heart attack or undergone heart surgery and have been forced to take a look at their lifestyle and make certain changes.

In the beginning, there are a lot of down faces! People seem to assume that it's going to be really difficult to cut their favourite things out of their diet and to eat healthily. The great news is that the majority of people find it much easier than they imagine. That's because being healthy is a really good thing. Yes, it's true you may have to change your dietary habits, but the upside is you'll begin to feel better than you ever thought you would.

This is something that I care deeply about. I wish that everyone could realize the benefits of being healthier. When you eat for nourishment, you have more energy and get up and go! Your skin tone will improve, so you'll look younger. Your mood will feel lighter and your brain sharper and, of course, you'll be helping your body to guard against heart attacks, strokes, diabetes and some cancers.

If you follow my philosophy, you'll be surprised how quickly you'll start to feel the benefits, even if you didn't realize you needed to make changes! And the better you feel, the more encouraged you'll be to continue on the path to a healthy diet and lifestyle.

spicy couscous

everyday

A lovely, exotic alternative to rice, this recipe works well on its own or as a side dish to accompany a green salad or a chicken or lamb dish.

serves 4

2 tbsp olive oil

1 garlic clove, peeled and crushed

1 tbsp ground cumin

1 tsp ground coriander

1 tsp paprika

350ml/12fl oz/1½ cups chicken or vegetable stock

good pinch of saffron strands

6 salad onions, trimmed and thinly sliced

225g/8oz/1⅓ cups couscous

coarsely grated zest and juice of 1 lemon

2 red chillies, deseeded and very finely chopped

2 tbsp raisins

2 tbsp pomegranate seeds (optional)

55g/2oz/⅓ cup pine nuts, toasted

1 Heat 1 tablespoon olive oil in a large, lidded pan over a medium heat. Add the garlic, cumin, coriander and paprika and fry over a gentle heat for 1 minute, stirring.

2 Add the stock and saffron and bring to the boil. Add the salad onions, and then pour in the couscous in a steady stream and give it a quick stir.

3 Cover the pan with a tight-fitting lid, remove from the heat and set aside for 5 minutes, to allow the grains to swell and absorb the stock.

4 If you are serving this warm, stir in the rest of the oil and the remaining ingredients now. Otherwise, leave the couscous to cool and chill in the refrigerator for 1 hour, then add all the other ingredients for a deliciously cold couscous salad.

egg and chips

treat

This isn't a dish that you would usually associate with heart-healthy food, but when made in this way using fresh oven-baked ingredients, it's a wonderfully nutritious dish. Tomatoes are a fantastic source of vitamins A and E, as well as potassium, beta-carotene and lycopene, which is thought to prevent certain cancers. The chips (thick fries) are oven-baked in just a little olive oil and are high in vitamin C and fibre; so this is an all-round nutritional meal that will feed a houseful, even on a budget.

1 Preheat the oven to 200°C/400°F/Gas mark 6.

2 After scrubbing the potatoes well but keeping the skins on (if organic), cut the potatoes lengthways into thick strips. Put in a roasting tin (preferably on a non-stick baking liner), then drizzle lightly with olive oil. Sprinkle with the salt substitute and bake for 20 minutes.

4 Meanwhile, cut the tomatoes in half and spread over the base of a large, shallow ovenproof dish.

5 Drizzle over the olive oil and sprinkle over the garlic slices, then add plenty of black pepper, the sugar and a dash of Worcestershire sauce.

6 After 20 minutes, take out the chips, and give them a big stir and shake around. Pop back into the oven along with the tomatoes. Leave both to cook for 40 minutes – checking halfway through cooking and turning the chips.

7 Take the tomatoes out of the oven, and with a wooden spoon make a large gap down the middle of the tomatoes. Quickly crack all 8 eggs into the gap and pop back into the oven for 5–6 minutes.

8 Take everything out of the oven, scatter the tomatoes with the herbs and serve piping hot.

serves 4 (2 eggs per person)

900g/2lb ripe vine tomatoes

3 tbsp extra-virgin olive oil

3 garlic cloves, peeled and finely sliced

freshly ground black pepper

2 tsp sugar

sprinkling of Worcestershire sauce

8 medium free-range eggs

2 tbsp chopped fresh flat-leaf parsley

2 tbsp chopped fresh chives

for the chips:

4 large organic white potatoes

drizzle of olive oil

a tiny amount of Maldon sea salt (see page 106)

italian blushing pasta

everyday

I like the simplicity of this pasta dish and you can really taste the sweetness of the tomatoes. However, if you like more sauce on your pasta, you can add a couple of teaspoons of pesto.

1 Preheat the oven to 190°C/375°F/Gas mark 5.

2 On a large baking tray, place all the vegetables. Do not peel the garlic bulb, but slice off the very top so that the cloves are just exposed. If you have a non-stick baking sheet, I recommend that you use it for this dish.

3 Drizzle everything with a little olive oil and dust over with the oregano, garlic powder, celery salt and black pepper. Make sure that everything is glistening with the oil and flavours but not drowning! Pop the fresh rosemary on top and put in the oven for about 50 minutes, checking and turning the peppers halfway through.

4 Meanwhile, organize your timings so that the pasta will be cooked at the same time as the vegetables. Dried pasta can take up to 20 minutes, whereas fresh pasta takes only 4–5 minutes, so follow the instructions on the packaging.

5 Drain the pasta very well and put in a big bowl. Add the vegetables and stir together, being careful not to break up the tomatoes. Squeeze the garlic out of its skin and add to dish.

6 Serve immediately with a fresh green salad.

serves 4 – but feel free to double up

about 20 cherry tomatoes, halved

2 red (bell) peppers, deseeded and cut into chunks

8 shallots, peeled and halved

1 whole garlic bulb, unpeeled

drizzle of olive oil

1 tsp dried oregano

1 tsp garlic powder

1 tsp celery salt

freshly ground black pepper

2–3 fresh rosemary sprigs

450g/1lb your choice of pasta

healthy spring vegetable risotto

everyday

If you feel tired and lethargic and need an energy boost, this is the perfect dish. It's incredibly filling because of the high fibre content and is jam-packed with long-lasting energy givers.

serves 4

1 litre/1¾ pints/4 cups vegetable stock

100g/3½oz asparagus tips

100g/3½oz baby carrots, halved lengthways

200g/7oz/2 cups fresh young peas, shelled

500g/1lb 2oz/4½ cups baby broad (fava) beans, shelled

2 tbsp olive oil

2 baby leeks, thinly sliced

300g/10½oz/1½ cups risotto rice

1 tbsp fresh pesto (store-bought is fine)

freshly ground black pepper

25g/1oz/scant ¼ cups pine nuts, toasted

1 Bring the stock to the boil in a large saucepan, then reduce the heat and add the asparagus tips, carrots, peas and broad (fava) beans and simmer for 4–5 minutes, or until tender.

2 Remove the vegetables with a draining spoon and set aside. Keep the stock simmering over a gentle heat.

3 Meanwhile, heat the oil in a large, heavy-based frying pan and add the leeks. Stir-fry for 2 minutes on a medium heat, or until they are bright green, then stir in the rice.

4 Add 2–3 tablespoons of the hot stock and cook gently, stirring until the liquid is absorbed. Continue adding the stock, a little at a time and stirring regularly, until the mixture is soupy and the grains of rice are tender but still have a slight bite. This will take about 20 minutes.

5 Stir in the pesto and season with black pepper to taste. Gently stir in the asparagus, carrots, peas and beans and cook for a few more minutes, or until the vegetables are heated through.

6 Serve in warmed dishes, sprinkled with the toasted pine nuts.

fragrant tomato filo tart

everyday

Tomatoes are extremely good for you. As well as being delicious, recent studies suggest that lycopene, the pigment that gives tomatoes their red colour, may help prevent some forms of cancer by lessening the damage caused by 'free radicals'. Tomatoes are also a valuable source of potassium (good for leg cramps), beta-carotene and vitamins C and E. This dish makes a lovely light lunch or a great starter.

serves 4

1 onion, peeled and thinly sliced

2 tbsp olive oil

4 sheets of filo (phyllo) pastry

½ tsp ground coriander

½ tsp fennel seeds

1 tsp cumin seeds

2 garlic cloves, peeled and sliced

½ tsp chilli powder

6 large ripe tomatoes, each cut into 4 thick slices

1 Preheat the oven and a non-stick baking tray to 220°C/425°F/Gas mark 7.

2 Put the sliced onions in a large, lidded frying pan with a drizzle of olive oil, cover and cook on a very low heat for 15-20 minutes, or until starting to caramelize.

3 Meanwhile, place the filo (phyllo) pastry sheets on top of each other on a non-stick baking tray.

4 When the onions have started to caramelize, add the coriander, fennel seeds, cumin and garlic, and stir-fry until the spices start releasing their wonderful fragrance.

5 Add the chilli powder and the tomatoes (you will need to do this in two batches), and cook for 1-2 minutes, being careful not to break up the tomato slices. Set aside any cooking juices.

6 As the tomato slices are cooked, arrange them on the pastry, leaving a 5mm/¼in edge to the pastry. Set the baking tray on top of the hot tray in the oven and cook for 15-20 minutes, or until the pastry is crisp and golden.

7 Drizzle any spicy tomato juices over the tart and serve.

chicken

aromatic chicken

everyday

The name says it all. Full of flavour and goodness. An easy everyday dish to tempt the taste-buds. Feel free to fill this dish out with extra veggies!

serves 4

2 tbsp coriander seeds

2 tsp cumin seeds

6 cloves

½ tsp freshly grated nutmeg

½ tsp ground turmeric

4 skinless chicken breast portions

1 onion, peeled and chopped

1 green (bell) pepper, chopped

2.5cm/1in fresh ginger root, peeled and sliced

300ml/10fl oz/1¼ cups hot homemade chicken stock or water

freshly ground black pepper

boiled rice, to serve

1 In a large non-stick frying pan, dry-fry the coriander, cumin and cloves for 2 minutes, or until the spices give off a good aroma. Add the nutmeg and turmeric and heat just for 1 more minute.

2 Remove the spices from the heat and grind together with the ginger in a pestle and mortar to make a paste.

3 Place the chicken breasts in a large, flameproof, lidded, casserole. Add the ground spices and ginger paste, the chopped onion and (bell) pepper and the chicken stock. Make sure the chicken is covered by the liquid. If it isn't, add a little more water.

4 Cover with a lid and cook over a gentle heat for about 45-50 minutes, or until the chicken pieces are really tender.

5 Season with pepper to taste, then serve portions of the chicken, with the sauce, on boiled rice.

fast food

I am always amazed by people's lack of imagination when it comes to 'fast food'. Instead of hitting the burger bar or fish and chip shop, or eating a chocolate bar or bag of crisps, try wholemeal (whole-wheat) pitta, popped in the toaster and dipped in low-fat hummus (see page 8). Or an omelette, which takes less that five minutes to prepare and cook! My kids love omelettes, and I'm happy for them to snack away on one whenever they fancy. Fast, simple food at its best.

We've all been caught hungry when out and about, but there are ways to keep healthy while eating fast! Here are a few hints and tips …

- Choose grilled (broiled) chicken instead of fried and go for a plain grilled hamburger without the cheese
- Steer clear of mayonnaise
- Go for wholemeal sandwiches instead of pastries and pies – again, skip the mayo
- Order a baked potato with beans or tuna, but no butter or mayo
- Air-cooked popcorn is better than fat-fried
- If eating at a restaurant, go for dry breadsticks instead of high-fat garlic bread
- At an Indian restaurant, ask for grilled poppadoms instead of fried ones and try to go for a tomato-based dish such as rogan josh or jalfrezi instead of a creamy korma. Avoid the oily side dishes like bhajis and samosas
- At a Chinese restaurant, go for boiled rice instead of fried and avoid the prawn crackers and fried starters. Instead, choose chicken and sweetcorn (corn) soup. For a main course, choose a vegetable- and chicken-based dish and avoid the high-fat crispy duck – and be sure to order your food without MSG! (Monosodium glutamate is a flavour enhancer that is very bad for your heart and which can cause palpitations in sensitive people.)
- If you have to go for fish and chips, take the batter off the fish and eat only a small portion of the chips

If you've had a day out and have eaten more of the fast food that you should have done – don't panic, just get out for a brisk walk or a bit of exercise to burn off the excess calories and watch what you eat the following day.

ratatouille chicken tray bake

everyday

This dish is just about as easy as they come yet tastes absolutely divine. Feel free to play with the quantities to add more of your favourite veggies! I prefer to use organic potatoes so that I can leave the skin on. All the goodness is just under the skin and it's much quicker to wash rather than peel them.

1 Preheat the oven to 200°C/400°F/Gas mark 6.

2 Mix the lemon zest with the herbs and crushed garlic. Lightly slash the chicken breasts using a sharp knife and rub the mixture all over and into the chicken.

3 Put the chicken, potatoes, leeks, (bell) peppers, parsnips and carrots in a large, deep roasting tin. Drizzle with olive oil and lemon juice. Season lightly with garlic powder, celery salt and black pepper.

4 Roast for 25 minutes, stir everything around, then add the cherry tomatoes and stir again so that everything browns evenly. Roast for a further 25-30 minutes, or until cooked through.

5 Check that the chicken is cooked through by piercing the thickest part of each breast with a sharp knife: the juices should run clear. Serve immediately.

Don't always assume that a 'healthy' meal has to be based on a salad. Sometimes we need comfort food to fill us up.

serves 4

zest and juice of 1 lemon

handful of fresh rosemary

sprinkling of fresh thyme

2 garlic cloves, peeled and crushed

4 skinless chicken breast portions

600g/1lb 5oz organic white potatoes, cut into wedges

4 leeks, rinsed and cut into four

1 green, 1 red and 1 yellow (bell) pepper, chopped

2 parsnips, peeled and quartered lengthways

2 carrots, cut into chunks

2–3 tbsp olive oil

½ tsp garlic powder

½ tsp celery salt (see page 106)

freshly ground black pepper

200g/7oz cherry tomatoes

chicken casserole

everyday

This dish is easy-peasy but so delicious my family demand it at least once a week. It's simple enough to have mid-week without too much fuss, with a good helping of brown or basmati rice and lots of green vegetables (I love it with steamed asparagus).

This recipe calls for white wine, which does give a lovely flavour. Most of the alcohol is burned off during cooking, so it's not a problem. However, if you'd like to miss out the wine, simply add more stock or even some non-alcoholic grape juice.

serves 4

2 tbsp plain (all-purpose) flour

freshly ground black pepper

sprinkling of dried mixed herbs

4–6 skinless chicken breast portions, cut into chunky pieces

2 tbsp extra virgin olive oil

6 rashers (slices) very lean bacon, cut into cubes

225g/8oz shallots, peeled, and halved if large

2 garlic cloves, peeled and crushed

2 courgettes (zucchini), sliced

1 red and 1 green (bell) pepper, deseeded and sliced

300ml/10fl oz/1¼ cups chicken or vegetable stock

300ml/10fl oz/1¼ cups white wine (the alcohol will burn off during cooking)

1 Preheat the oven to 160ºC/325ºF/Gas mark 3.

2 Mix the plain (all-purpose) flour with some black pepper and the dried mixed herbs in a large bowl, then dust the chicken breasts in the flour and put to one side. Reserve some flour for the sauce.

3 Over a medium heat, gently heat the olive oil in a large, lidded flameproof casserole dish. Add the chicken and the bacon and fry until golden.

4 Add the shallots and garlic and sauté for 2–3 minutes, or until softened.

5 Now add all the remaining ingredients – the (bell) peppers, courgettes (zucchini), stock and wine. Stir in the reserved flour to add thickness to the sauce.

6 Cover and cook in the oven for about 1½ hours, or until the chicken is nice and tender.

If towards the end of cooking you feel the sauce has reduced too much, just add a little more stock.

chicken chilli burgers

everyday

With no added fat, these are spicy, healthy burgers to tempt your tastebuds. You could always make these into mini meatballs instead and serve with a green salad if you don't want to have bread with them.

1 In a large bowl, mix together the minced (ground) chicken, onion, garlic, chilli, herbs, Worcestershire sauce and plenty of black pepper. Then shape the mixture into four even-sized burgers.

2 Preheat the grill (broiler) to medium. Or prepare your barbecue (grill).

3 Grill the burgers, or cook on the barbecue, for 5–6 minutes on each side – until well browned and cooked through.

4 Serve in the burger buns with rocket (arugula) and juicy, sliced tomatoes.

You don't always need to use salt or fat to add flavour to a dish – herbs and spices work just as well and are better for you.

serves 4

450g/1lb lean minced (ground) chicken or turkey

1 small onion, peeled and finely chopped

2 garlic cloves, crushed

1 red chilli, deseeded and finely chopped

2 handfuls chopped fresh flat-leaf parsley

2 tsp Worcestershire sauce

freshly ground black pepper

to serve:

wholemeal (whole-wheat) burger buns, sliced in half

rocket (arugula) and tomato slices

magnificent moroccan chicken

everyday

This recipe was inspired by my good Moroccan friend Mida. Traditionally, this dish is made using preserved lemons. Though you could use fresh, the preserved ones give that authentic Moroccan flavour. They can usually be found in any of the big supermarkets or a good local deli.

serves 4–6

1 chicken, 1.3–1.8kg/3–4lb, cut into 8 pieces and skinned (or 6 chicken breast portions)

2 tsp paprika

1 tsp ground cumin

1 tsp ground ginger

1 tsp turmeric

1 tsp cinnamon

freshly ground black pepper

2 tbsp olive oil

3 garlic cloves, minced

1 onion, peeled and finely sliced

1 glass of white wine

2 preserved lemons, rinsed in cold water and halved, or 2 fresh lemons, washed and halved

175g/6oz/1 cup green olives, pitted

120g/4½ cup canned chickpeas

75g/3oz/½ cup raisins

600ml/1 pint/2½ cups chicken or vegetable stock

handful of chopped fresh coriander (cilantro)

handful of chopped parsley

1 Pat dry the chicken pieces. Combine all the spices in a large bowl, then add the chicken pieces to coat well with the spice mixture. Let the chicken marinate for 1 hour in the spices.

2 In a large frying pan or non-stick saucepan with a lid, heat the olive oil over medium-high heat. Add the chicken pieces and cook for 7 minutes, or until browned on all sides. Lower the heat to medium-low, then add the garlic and onion. Cover and cook for 15 minutes.

3 Add the white wine (the alcohol will evaporate), lemon halves, olives, chickpeas, raisins and stock. Bring to a simmer over a medium heat, then reduce the heat to low, cover, and cook for an additional 35–45 minutes, stirring regularly, until the chicken is cooked through and tender.

4 Mix in the chopped coriander and parsley, then serve immediately.

5 Serve with Spicy Couscous (see page 38) or rice.

thai chicken stir-fry

everyday

Oriental fast food! This recipe takes 10 minutes from start to finish and is delicious. I sometimes cook it in advance and eat it cold as a packed lunch. This makes a lovely light dish without the carbohydrate. If you want to fill it out more, serve with boiled rice or egg noodles.

serves 1 – but increase the quantities to feed more people

1 tbsp olive oil

1 skinless chicken breast portion, sliced very thinly

1 medium carrot, cut into matchstick shapes

2 spring onions (scallions), sliced

½ medium red, green or yellow (bell) pepper, deseeded and thinly sliced

1 tbsp soy sauce

½ level tsp cornflour (cornstarch)

4 tbsp water

½ tsp grated ginger root

1 tbsp sesame seeds, to serve

1 In a non-stick frying pan or wok over a medium heat, heat the oil and then stir-fry the chicken and vegetables for 5 minutes.

2 Mix together the remaining ingredients (except the sesame seeds) in a cup and add to the pan. Mix in well and cook for 2–3 minutes, stirring constantly.

3 Finally, sprinkle over the sesame seeds and serve.

It's very easy to make a meal stretch if you suddenly have extra mouths to feed, or you may just want to make a light dish more substantial. Most recipes can easily be doubled or you can just add an extra handful of vegetables, beans, pasta or rice.

chicken risotto parcel

everyday

A 'ready meal' with none of the hidden salt or sugar. You can chuck all the raw ingredients in the foil parcel (pocket) in the morning, pop it in the refrigerator and then just bung it in the oven when you get home from work. You can then unwind for an hour, have a soak in the bath, chat on the phone – and 'ping' the timer goes off and you have the most delicious, nutritious ready meal!

1. Preheat the oven to 400°F/200°C/Gas mark 6.

2. Prepare a large piece of foil by folding it in half to give extra strength.

3. Mix all the ingredients together in a large bowl.

4. Pile all the ingredients into the centre of the foil. Fold up the sides to produce a bowl effect and fold over the top to seal the edges securely.

5. Place on a baking sheet and cook for 45 minutes, or until the chicken is cooked through and the rice has absorbed the stock.

serves 1 – but make as many as you like

1 skinless chicken breast portion

4–5 mushrooms, sliced

4–5 cherry tomatoes

¼ onion, finely chopped

drizzle of olive oil

40g/1½oz/scant ½ cup long-grain rice

200ml/7fl oz / ⅔ cup chicken stock

1 tbsp tomato purée (paste)

dash of Worcestershire sauce

sprinkling of chopped fresh or dried mixed herbs (e.g. thyme, parsley or oregano)

sprinkling of garlic powder

freshly ground black pepper

quick cajun chicken salad

everyday

You can make this into a more filling meal by serving it with rice or pasta.

serves 4

4 good-sized skinless chicken breast portions

2 tbsp cajun spice mix

drizzle of olive oil

fresh salad leaves

lemon wedges, to serve

1 Cut each chicken breast in half lengthways and dust with the cajun chicken spices. Leave to marinate for 10 minutes in the refrigerator to get the full flavour.

2 In a large frying pan, drizzle a little olive oil and cook the chicken for 7–8 minutes, turning halfway through, ensuring that the pieces are cooked thoroughly all the way through.

3 Serve on a bed of green leaves with the lemon wedges.

chicken curry with sweet onions

everyday

This dish is very mild and makes a delicious introduction to curry for children. Once they get used to the flavour, you can easily spice it up a little more by adding extra curry powder. The apple juice gives a lovely sweetness.

serves 4

2 tbsp olive oil

3 onions, peeled and thinly sliced

2 green (bell) peppers, peeled and very finely sliced

2 garlic cloves, peeled and finely chopped

2 tbsp plain (all-purpose) flour

freshly ground black pepper

1 tsp dried mixed herbs

1 tsp mild curry powder

4 skinless chicken breast portions each cut into chunks

300ml/10floz/1¼ cups unsweetened apple juice

2 tbsp tomato purée (paste)

chopped fresh flat-leaf parsley or coriander, to garnish

1. In a large, lidded frying pan, heat the oil over a medium heat and add the onions and green (bell) peppers and stir well.

2. Cook gently for 15 minutes, or until the onions are starting to soften and caramelize.

3. Add the garlic and cook for another 5 minutes, stirring well again. Take the onion and garlic mixture out of the pan and put to one side in a small bowl.

4. In a separate, larger bowl, mix together the flour, black pepper, herbs and curry powder. Cover the chicken pieces in the flour mixture and shake off any excess.

5. Over a high heat, cook the chicken in the frying pan (with a dash of extra olive oil if needed) for about 5 minutes. Turn, and cook for a further 5 minutes to brown all over.

6. Pour in the apple juice and add the tomato purée (paste). Stir really well to incorporate all of the flavours. Next return the onions and peppers to the pan, cover with a lid and cook for about 25 minutes.

7. Check that the chicken is cooked right through. Sprinkle with a little parsley or coriander (cilantro), then serve with basmati or wild rice.

fish

smoked haddock kedgeree
treat

Smoked haddock does contain salt, so this isn't a dish for every day. If you love fish, this is very filling, and a healthier alternative to a fish pie.

serves 4

300g/11oz un-dyed smoked haddock fillet

1 bay leaf

1½ pints/3½fl oz/3¾ cups vegetable stock, hot

1 tbsp olive oil

2 shallots, peeled and finely chopped

½ tsp ground cumin

½ tsp ground coriander

1 tsp mild curry powder

300g/10½oz/1½ cups basmati rice, rinsed

small strip of lemon zest and 1 tbsp lemon juice

150g/5½oz/1½ cups fresh or frozen peas

4 tomatoes, chopped

2 tbsp snipped fresh chives, plus extra to garnish

freshly ground black pepper

2 medium-sized hardboiled eggs, to serve

slices of lemon, to garnish (optional)

1 Put the smoked haddock in a large deep, lidded frying pan. Add the bay leaf, then pour over the stock. Heat to simmering point, then reduce the heat, half-cover the pan with the lid and poach for 6–8 minutes, or until the flesh flakes easily when tested with the tip of a knife. Lift the fish out of the cooking liquid and set aside.

2 Make up the volume of the cooking liquid to 600ml/1 pint/2½ cups with water and put to one side with the bay leaf.

3 Rinse out the frying pan, then add the oil and heat over a moderate heat for a few seconds.

4 Add the shallots and cook for 4–5 minutes, or until softened, then stir in the spices, followed by the rice. Stir for a few seconds to coat with the oil and spices, then add the reserved cooking liquid and bay leaf and the strip of lemon zest. Bring to the boil. Reduce the heat to a gentle simmer, then cover and cook for 10 minutes.

5 Add the peas, cover again and cook for a further 5 minutes, or until the rice is tender and nearly all the stock is absorbed.

6 Meanwhile, flake the fish, removing any skin and bones. Reduce the heat under the pan to very low, then gently stir the fish into the rice together with the tomatoes, lemon juice and chives.

7 Season with black pepper to taste, then transfer the kedgeree to a warm serving dish and garnish with egg quarters, extra chives and lemon slices.

smoked haddock chowder

everyday

This is a healthier version of a traditional chowder because it's thickened with creamed sweetcorn (corn) rather than dairy cream. It's great to put in a flask and eat on the go on a chilly day.

1 Put the onion, garlic and potatoes into a large frying pan. Pour over the vegetable stock and simmer for about 8 minutes, or until the potatoes are soft but still have a slight bite.

2 Add the chunks of smoked haddock, the creamed corn and half of the milk – if you prefer thinner chowder, add more. Season with a little black pepper.

3 Gently simmer for 5–7 minutes, or until the haddock is cooked (it should flake easily when pressed with a fork).

4 Sprinkle over the parsley and serve with chunky wholemeal bread.

Pollock, monkfish (angler fish) or cod would also work well in this dish.

serves 2

1 onion, chopped

1 garlic clove, peeled and crushed

2 potatoes, scrubbed and sliced

500ml/18fl oz/generous 2 cups vegetable stock

2 smoked haddock fillets, about 115g/4oz each, skinned and cut into chunks

400g/14oz canned creamed sweetcorn (corn)

4 tbsp semi-skimmed (low-fat) milk, or to taste

freshly ground black pepper

handful fresh flat-leaf parsley, chopped, to garnish

peppered lemony monkfish
everyday

Try serving with a sachet of 'express rice'. Great if you're in a hurry!

serves 4

500g/1lb 2oz monkfish (angler fish) fillet, skinned and cut into 4cm/1½in chunks

1 tbsp Black Pepper and Garlic Crush (see page 106)

2 tbsp olive oil

1 onion, peeled and finely sliced

2 red and 2 yellow (bell) peppers, deseeded and thinly sliced

175g/6oz/2 cups sugarsnap peas, halved lengthways

grated zest and juice of 1 lemon

handful of fresh basil, torn, to garnish

1 Place the monkfish (angler fish) chunks in a bowl with the black pepper and garlic crush. Marinate for 10 minutes or so.

2 Heat a wok or large frying pan over a high heat and add 1 tablespoon vegetable oil. Add the onion and stir-fry for 1 minute. Stir in the (bell) peppers and sugarsnap peas and continue stir-frying for about 5 minutes. Remove the vegetables to a plate using a slotted spoon.

3 Add the remaining oil to the pan, then add the marinated monkfish and stir-fry on a gentle heat for about 4 minutes, carefully turning the chunks so as not to break them up, until the fish is cooked through and flakes easily.

4 Add the lemon zest and juice, and return the stir-fried vegetables to the pan to heat through, stirring for 2-3 minutes. Scatter over the basil and serve at once on a bed of rice.

Try to buy unwaxed lemons, especially for grating.

seared scallops with butternut and parsley mash

everyday

This makes a healthy dinner party dish. You can prepare the mashed potato in advance and just reheat in a microwave. And as the scallops take only minutes to cook, you'll still have plenty of time to entertain your guests.

1 Put the scallops into a shallow, non-metallic bowl with the lime zest and juice, ginger and soy sauce. Stir well, then cover and marinate for 20 minutes.

2 Meanwhile, bring a large saucepan of water to the boil. Then cook the butternut squash and potatoes for about 20 minutes, or until tender.

3 Drain the potatoes well and mash thoroughly, then beat in the low-fat soft cheese. Season with black pepper. Keep warm over a very low heat, stirring occasionally.

4 Heat a griddle pan or non-stick frying pan. Drain the scallops and add to the pan. Cook for about 1 minute on each side. Avoid overcooking them, as they can quickly toughen.

5 Share the mash between two warmed plates and serve with the scallops, garnished with sprigs of chervil or lemon thyme.

serves 2

250g/9oz scallops

juice and zest (finely grated) from 1 lime

1 tsp finely grated fresh ginger root

2 tbsp soy sauce

350g/12oz butternut squash, peeled, deseeded and cut into chunks

350g/12oz potatoes, peeled and cut into chunks

55g/2oz/¼ cup low-fat soft cheese

freshly ground black pepper

sprig of fresh lemon thyme or chervil, to garnish

dani's marinated seabass on a bed of noodles

everyday

Dani is one of my very best gorgeous girlfriends. She loves to entertain and cooks up a storm for us all at the drop of a hat. This is a dish she taught me to do and it's delicious!

serves 2

2 small seabass fillets, about 900g–1kg/2lb–2lb 4oz total weight

400g/14oz packet fresh egg noodles

fresh flat-leaf parsley, to garnish (optional)

for the marinade:

1 small onion, peeled and diced

1 small fresh red chilli, deseeded and diced

1 garlic clove, peeled and crushed

½ tsp ground coriander

½ tsp ground cumin

2.5cm/1in fresh ginger root, peeled and finely grated

1 tbsp clear honey

juice of 1 lemon

2 tbsp olive oil

freshly ground black pepper

1　Rinse and dry the fish fillets. Place the marinade ingredients into a shallow dish and mix together, then add the fish and cover with the marinade. Cover the dish and leave in the refrigerator for up to 2 hours if possible.

2　Preheat the oven to 220ºC/425ºF/Gas mark 7. Line a roasting tin with enough foil to make a generous envelope. Grease the foil with a little olive oil, then add the seabass fillets and any remaining marinade. Fold over the edges of the foil to create a puffed-up, sealed envelope and bake the fish for 20 minutes, or until the flesh is firm. Remove from the oven and leave to rest for a further 3 minutes.

3　While the fish rests, cook the fresh noodles in boiling water as per the packet instructions (usually about 3 minutes).

4　Remove the fish from the foil and arrange on warmed serving plates on top of the noodles. Pour over any remaining cooking juices, garnish with parsley and serve.

sardines on toast

everyday

Sardines are packed with goodness, such as omega-3 fatty acids, protein, iron and zinc, and make a really quick and easy snack. We used to have them for Sunday supper sometimes – either that or toasted crumpets with butter. However, no matter how hard I try, I cannot come up with a suitably healthy version of buttered crumpets, so sardines on toast it is!

1 Lightly break up the sardines in a medium-sized bowl with a fork. Add the chopped celery, red (bell) pepper, spring onion (scallion), tomato purée and lime juice to the sardines. Season lightly with celery salt and freshly ground black pepper.

2 Toast the bread slices on both sides until golden.

3 Spoon the sardine mixture over the toast to make an open sandwich and add the olives or watercress to garnish. Serve immediately.

Feel free to swap the sardines for pilchards.

serves 4

120g/4½oz can sardines in tomato sauce

1 celery stick, finely chopped

½ red (bell) pepper, deseeded and finely chopped

1 spring onion (scallion), thinly sliced

1 tbsp sun-dried tomato purée (paste)

2 tbsp lime juice

celery salt (see page 106)

freshly ground black pepper

4 thick slices of wholemeal (whole-wheat) or multigrain bread

olives or a watercress sprig, to garnish

snappy tuna melt

everyday

This dish is as easy as they come, but so perfectly tasty! Canned tuna is rich in vitamins D and B12. 'Melts' usually contain a lot of cheese, but this dish is delicious with just a tiny amount, or none at all. Why not add a couple of slices of avocado on top if you feel the need for a more substantial meal?

1 Toast the chunky wholemeal (whole-wheat) bread on both sides – put to one side.

2 Heat the olive oil in a medium-sized pan over a moderate heat, then sauté the garlic, spring onions, and (bell) pepper. Cook for 5-6 minutes, or until soft.

3 Add the chopped tomatoes, tuna and some black pepper, then cook for another 3-4 minutes, or until heated through.

4 Pile the tuna mixture on the toast, adding the avocado slices or grated cheese (if using).

5 Pop under a hot grill (broiler) for just a couple of minutes to melt together. Serve with watercress or mixed salad leaves and cucumber ribbons. Lovely!

serves 2

2 slices of nutty wholemeal (whole-wheat) chunky bread

1 tbsp olive oil

1 garlic clove, peeled and crushed

2 spring onions (scallions), thinly sliced

1 red (bell) pepper, deseeded and finely diced

2 tomatoes, very finely chopped

2 x 160g cans tuna in spring water, drained

freshly ground black pepper

½ avocado, sliced, or 2 tsp grated cheese (optional)

to serve:

watercress or mixed salad leaves (greens)

½ cucumber, sliced in ribbons

tuna kebabs
with roast baby carrots and baby courgettes

everyday

These kebabs are high intensity in the taste stakes, and look impressive if you are serving up for friends. Low in fat and high in protein. Perfect!

serves 4

2 tsp whole black peppercorns

2 garlic cloves, peeled

fresh rosemary sprig

juice of 1 lemon

extra-virgin olive oil

2 large fresh tuna steaks

1 glass white wine (125ml/ 4fl oz/½ cup)

for the vegetables:

200g/7oz baby carrots, topped and tailed

200g/7oz baby courgettes (zucchini)

drizzle of olive oil

celery salt (see page 106)

garlic powder

4 wooden skewers

1 Preheat the oven to 200ºC/400ºF/Gas mark 6. Soak the skewers in water; this will prevent them from splintering and should stop them from burning during cooking.

2 Pop the baby vegetables in a roasting tray. Drizzle with a little olive oil. Sprinkle with a dusting of celery salt and garlic powder and put in the oven for about 40 minutes.

3 Meanwhile, cut the tuna steaks into chunks - about 1.5cm/ ⅝in square.

4 In a pestle and mortar, crush the black peppercorns together with the garlic, rosemary and lemon juice. Put this in a large bowl together with the tuna and mix up well so that all the fish is covered.

5 Thread the cubes of fish onto the skewers.

6 Next, heat up a little olive oil in a large frying pan over a medium heat, carefully place the kebabs into the pan and cook for 7-8 minutes, turning so that all sides get nice and brown.

7 Put the kebabs to one side while you deglaze the pan with the glass of white wine (the alcohol will burn off). To do this, simply pour in the wine, turn up to a high heat and scrape the frying pan to get all the scrummy bits from the bottom of the pan.

8 Serve the kebabs on top of the roast vegetables, pouring over the wine glaze to finish off. Perfect with a helping of basmati rice (microwave Express Rice is fine!).

caribbean fish stew

everyday

My fish stew has a strong distinctive flavour and is really easy to make. You can leave out the rum if you prefer, but it does add to the rich taste.

1 Spread the lime zest and juice over the base of a 33 x 23cm/13 x 9in shallow dish. Lay the fish in the dish and pour over the lime juice.

2 Using a mortar and pestle, crush the thyme leaves, black peppercorns and 1 tablespoon of olive oil to make a paste. Rub the paste all over the fish and then sprinkle over the rum. Cover and marinate in the fridge for about 1 hour.

3 Heat the remaining olive oil in a large deep saucepan and fry the onion for 4-5 minutes, or until soft. Add the chopped parsley, garlic and sugar and cook for about 4 minutes.

4 Now add the tomato, prawns (shrimp) and the fish with the marinade to the pan. Pour over the stock and tomato purée (paste) and cook gently for 8-10 minutes, or until the fish is cooked through and flakes easily.

5 Season with a little more black pepper and serve with the lime halves and some chunky wholemeal (whole-wheat) bread.

serves 4

grated zest and juice of 1 lime

2 x 175–225g/6–8oz skinless white fish fillets such as cod, haddock or hoki

handful of fresh thyme, leaves picked

½ tsp black peppercorns

3 tbsp olive oil

1 tbsp dark rum (optional)

1 onion, peeled and cut into rings

handful of fresh flat-leaf parsley, chopped

2 garlic cloves, crushed

2 tsp dark muscovado sugar

1 beef (beefsteak) tomato (or equivalent smaller ones), sliced

6 cooked king prawns (jumbo shrimp)

300ml/10fl oz/1¼ cups vegetable stock

3 tbsp tomato purée (paste)

freshly ground black pepper

fresh lime halves, to serve

fish in a bag

everyday

This is the perfect, healthy 'ready meal'. Prepare it before work, store in the refrigerator and then cook it when you get home.

200g/7oz white fish fillets, skinned (cod or haddock or hake – whatever takes your fancy!)

juice of ½ lemon

1 tbsp olive oil

handful of flat-leaf parsley, roughly chopped

1 garlic clove, peeled and sliced or crushed

2 sage leaves

1 rosemary sprig

1 bay leaf

50ml/2fl oz/¼ cup white wine vinegar

freshly ground black pepper

1 Preheat the oven to 150°C/300°F/Gas mark 2.

2 Place the fish fillet on a large, double-thickness square of foil and drizzle over the lemon juice and olive oil.

3 Place all the other ingredients over the fish and wrap in the foil to make a securely sealed parcel. Bake for 20–25 minutes or until the fish is cooked through.

beef, lamb & pork

mediterranean beefburgers with red-hot tomato salsa

everyday*

These burgers taste best cooked outside on the barbecue. However, you can still make wonderful, healthy burgers by cooking them in a non-stick frying pan or griddle pan (no need to add any oil) or under a grill (broiler). The best option, though, is to use a George Foreman-style grill; all the fat runs out and you still get that 'chargrilled' effect.

Make sure you buy good-quality, lean minced beef. Remember that in moderation, a little red meat is good for a healthy diet as it helps top up your iron and zinc levels. However, if you've already had a meal with red meat this week, you can make this with chicken or turkey mince. The accompanying tomato salsa contains healthy antioxidants. Serve with a big green salad for a dish that's good for your health and your tastebuds!

serves 4

500g/1lb 2oz lean minced (ground) beef

25g/1oz/½ cup wholemeal (whole-wheat) breadcrumbs

2 garlic cloves, peeled and crushed

40g/1½oz/scant ⅓ cup sun-dried tomatoes in oil, drained and finely chopped

2 tbsp chopped fresh coriander (cilantro)

4 wholemeal (whole-wheat) burger buns

55g/2oz rocket (arugula)

continued opposite

1 Place the minced (ground) beef, breadcrumbs, garlic, chopped sun-dried tomatoes and coriander (cilantro) in a large bowl and use your hands to mix the ingredients together thoroughly.

2 Divide the mixture equally into 4 and shape into burgers about 10cm/4in across and a similar size to the buns.

3 In a frying pan or grill pan cook on a hot hob (stove). Alternatively, use a barbecue or George Foreman-style grill. Cook the burgers – either in a non-stick frying pan or griddle pan or on a barbecue – until nice and crispy on the outside and fully cooked on the inside.

4 To make the salsa, mix together all the ingredients in a medium-sized bowl. You can chop all the salsa ingredients together in a food processor to save time – just use the pulse button to get the right consistency.

5 Split the buns in half and pop under the grill (broiler) or onto the barbecue rack to toast lightly. Place a few rocket (arugula) leaves on each base, top with a burger and add a spoonful of salsa, then replace the tops. Serve immediately.

* red meat should only be eaten once or twice a week

for the tomato salsa:

225g/8oz ripe vine tomatoes, finely diced

1 red (bell) pepper, deseeded and finely diced

½ fresh mild green chilli, deseeded and finely chopped

1 fresh red chilli, deseeded and finely chopped

2 tsp balsamic vinegar

1 tbsp snipped fresh chives

1 tbsp chopped fresh coriander (cilantro)

meatballs in spicy
tomato and vegetable sauce

everyday*

This is a fantastic dish that you can easily increase to feed a houseful. Serve it with baked potatoes, wholemeal pasta or rice. It's a firm family favourite.

If you are feeding only one or two people, cool the remaining meatballs in the refrigerator and then freeze in suitable portion sizes. When you next fancy some meatballs, thaw out and re-heat the meatballs and sauce in a saucepan over a medium heat, ensuring the meatballs are properly heated all the way through.

A little red meat is good for you but not everyday – try chicken or turkey mince instead. Buy only lean mincemeat and don't over-eat. The meatball sauce here is jam-packed with nutrients from all the lovely vegetables, so you can happily enjoy a modest serving of this dish, guilt free.

1 Preheat the oven to 180°C/350°F/Gas mark 4.

2 To make the meatballs, put the steak mince (ground beef), chopped onions, garlic, egg, mustard, spices and parsley into a large bowl and mix together well. (Using your hands is usually the easiest way.) Divide the mixture into 8–10 pieces and shape into balls.

3 In a large, heavy-based saucepan, sauté the meatballs in a dash of olive oil over a medium heat, for about 15 minutes. Transfer them to a plate and keep warm in a low oven.

continued overleaf

serves 4

450g/1lb lean steak mince (ground lean beef)

2 onions, peeled and finely chopped

3 garlic cloves, peeled and finely chopped

1 egg, beaten

1 tsp Dijon mustard

1 tsp ground allspice

1 tsp ground cinnamon

freshly ground black pepper

a handful of fresh parsley, chopped

drizzle of olive oil, for frying

continued overleaf

4 To make the sauce, heat the olive oil in a saucepan and sauté the onion and garlic until softened. Add the finely chopped courgettes (zucchini) and (bell) peppers and sauté for a further 10 minutes, stirring occasionally. Add the tomatoes, and all remaining ingredients, and simmer for about 10 minutes.

5 Pour the sauce into a large casserole dish. Arrange the meatballs in the sauce, cover and cook in the oven for 20 minutes, or until the sauce is bubbling and the meatballs are piping hot. Garnish with the basil leaves and serve immediately.

red meat should only be enjoyed once or twice a week

Remember: If I can make these dishes, you can make them too. There may be an ingredient that you don't recognize, but give it a go - you just might love it!

for the sauce:

2 tbsp olive oil

1 large onion, peeled and finely chopped

2 garlic cloves, peeled and finely chopped

3 courgettes (zucchini), finely chopped

2 large red (bell) peppers, finely chopped

3 x 400g/14oz cans chopped tomatoes

1 tbsp Worcestershire sauce

1 tbsp balsamic vinegar

1 tesp dried oregano

handful of basil leaves, torn, to garnish

chilli con healthy

everyday*

If you go overboard on the fresh chilli, a dollop of low-fat natural yogurt or crème fraîche on the top is extremely tasty and it's a great way to cool things down!

serves 4

450g/1lb/3 cups extra lean minced (ground) beef

extra-virgin olive oil

1 large onion, peeled and finely chopped

2 garlic cloves, peeled and crushed

2 fresh chillies, deseeded and chopped

2 tsp ground cumin

1 tsp ground coriander

1 tsp paprika

pinch of cayenne pepper

400g/14oz can chopped tomatoes

1 level tbsp tomato purée (paste)

600ml/1 pint/2½ cups beef stock

freshly ground black pepper

400g/14oz can red kidney beans, drained

chopped fresh coriander (cilantro), to serve

low-fat natural yogurt or crème fraîche (optional), to serve

1 In a large, lidded saucepan, dry-fry the minced (ground) beef until brown over a high heat. Drain off any fat. Turn down to a medium-low heat and add a splash of olive oil and then add the onion and garlic and cook gently until softened.

2 Add the chillies and all the spices and continue frying, stirring occasionally, for 2–3 minutes.

3 Add the canned tomatoes, tomato purée (paste) and stock. Stir well and bring to the boil. Reduce the heat and simmer gently for 15 minutes, or until the liquid is slightly reduced.

4 Season with pepper and add the drained kidney beans. Cover and heat through gently for another 30 minutes, adding a little extra stock if required.

5 Serve hot, sprinkled with chopped coriander (cilantro) leaves and a dollop of yogurt or crème fraîche (if using), and accompanied by basmati rice or a fresh green salad.

* red meat should only be eaten once or twice a week. Try cooking this recipe with chicken or turkey mince instead.

healthiest-ever lasagne
*everyday**

This is a delicious, warming and rich lasagne without the added fat of a traditional lasagne. It's made without the usual fat-laden cheese sauce and only has a light sprinkling of cheese on top. Using very lean meat and only a tiny amount of olive oil, you can enjoy this dish with the family and feel happy that you are nourishing them wonderfully.

1 Heat the oil in a large, lidded saucepan over a low heat. Add the onion and fry gently for 5 minutes. Add the carrots, celery and garlic and cook for a further 5 minutes, or until the onion is soft and just beginning to colour.

2 Turn up the heat a little, then add the beef or turkey and cook, stirring and breaking up the meat with a wooden spoon, until browned and crumbly. Add the mushrooms and cook for 1 more minute, then drain off any fat from the meat.

3 Stir in the stock, wine or extra stock, tomatoes, tomato purée (paste) and dried herbs. Bring to the boil, then cover and gently simmer over a low heat for 45 minutes, stirring occasionally. Stir in the parsley and season with black pepper to taste.

4 Preheat the oven to 200°C/400°F/Gas mark 6.

5 To make the sauce, mix the cornflour (cornstarch) in a small bowl or cup to a smooth paste with a little of the milk. Add more milk until all the

continued overleaf

serves 4

2 tbsp extra-virgin olive oil

1 large onion, peeled and finely chopped

4 carrots, scrubbed but skin on and finely chopped (if you use organic, you can leave the skin on; if your carrots are not organic, I suggest you peel them)

2 organic celery sticks, finely chopped

2 garlic cloves, peeled and crushed

350g/12oz lean minced (ground) steak or turkey mince (ground turkey)

150g/5½oz chopped mushrooms, chopped

300ml/10fl oz/1¼ cups beef or chicken stock

150ml/5fl oz/⅔ cup red wine or extra stock

400g/14oz can chopped tomatoes

4 tbsp tomato purée (paste)

continued overleaf

1 tbsp dried oregano or
mixed herbs

freshly ground black pepper

handful of fresh flat-leaf
parsley, chopped

10–12 sheets dried
no-pre-cook lasagne

40g/1½oz mature low-fat
Cheddar cheese

for the sauce:

3 tbsp cornflour (cornstarch)

600ml/1 pint/2½ cups semi-
skimmed (low-fat) milk

pinch of freshly grated nutmeg

cornflour (cornstarch) has been dissolved and it is a runny consistency. Now put the cornflour (cornstarch) mixture along with the remaining milk into a medium-sized saucepan. Over a medium heat, bring to the boil while stirring continuously. Simmer for 2 minutes and stir in the nutmeg. The sauce should have thickened to a custard consistency. Take off the heat.

6 Spoon half the meat sauce over the base of a 3 litre/2¼ quart ovenproof dish or roasting tin. Cover with a layer of lasagne, then spoon over the remaining meat sauce and cover with another layer of pasta.

7 Pour over the white sauce to cover the lasagne completely. Scatter over the grated cheese.

8 Place the dish on a baking sheet and bake for 40–45 minutes, or until the lasagne is bubbling and the top is lightly browned. Remove from the oven and leave to settle for 10 minutes before serving. Accompany with a lovely big salad.

red meat should only be eaten once or twice a week

hearty shepherd's pie

everyday*

Shepherd's pie is an old tradition in many households and this is a version of my mother's recipe. As always, ensure you use great-quality, very lean minced beef. Red meat contains iron and zinc and this is complemented by the vitamin C and fibre content of the potato and sweet potato topping. The onions, garlic and tomatoes will help lower blood cholesterol making this dish a lovely, filling, nutritious meal.

1. Boil the potatoes and sweet potatoes for 15-20 minutes, or until tender.

2. Drain the potatoes, then mash with the milk using an electric whisk until smooth. Season with pepper.

3. In a large pan over a medium heat, dry-fry the minced (ground) lamb, beef or turkey until browned. Drain off any excess fat, then add the onion, celery and garlic and fry for a further 3-4 minutes, stirring occasionally.

4. Sprinkle over the flour and stir until the meat and onion mixture is evenly coated.

5. Add the canned tomatoes, vegetable stock, Worcestershire sauce and herbs. Bring to the boil, stirring until thickened. Reduce the heat, then cover and simmer for 20 minutes, stirring occasionally.

continued overleaf

serves 4-5

600g/1lb 5oz white, floury (mealy) potatoes, peeled and diced

600g/1lb 5oz sweet potatoes, peeled and diced

freshly ground black pepper, to taste

3 tbsp semi-skimmed (low-fat) milk

400g/14oz extra-lean minced (ground) lamb or beef or turkey.

1 medium onion, peeled and chopped

1 celery stick, chopped

2 garlic cloves, peeled and crushed or chopped

2 tsp plain (all-purpose) flour

450g/1lb canned chopped tomatoes

300ml/10fl oz/1 cups vegetable stock

continued overleaf

1 slug of Worcestershire sauce

2 bay leaves

handful of fresh rosemary,
leaves picked and chopped

handful of fresh oregano,
chopped, or a good sprinkling
of dried herbs if fresh not
available

6 Place the meat in an ovenproof dish. Spoon the mashed potato mixture over the top. and texture the topping with a fork.

7 Either grill (broil) until lightly browned, or pop into a preheated oven (200°C/400°F/Gas mark 6) for 20 minutes.

red meat should only be eaten once or twice a week

super mashed potato

Many traditional English dishes involve mashed potato - like bangers and mash, shepherd's pie and fish pie. Creamy mashed potato is warm and comforting, and my children love it just on its own with lots of gorgeous onion gravy (see page 112). You can see from the recipe that I don't add any butter or salt to the mash. Butter really isn't necessary if you use plenty of sweet potatoes, which are much softer and therefore hold their moisture better than white potatoes. All you need to do is add a splash of milk and, by using an electric whisk, you will get lovely fluffy light mashed potato with hardly any fat content.

You can add many things to flavour the mash, such as wholegrain mustard, rosemary, oregano, thyme, spring onions (scallions) or caramelized onions. Fennel and cumin seeds give a really exotic taste. Give it a go!

feeding children

Believe it or not, today's children are the first generation to be classed as unhealthy due to obesity. It is too easy for them to eat foods with a low nutritional value and containing 'empty calories' – calories which give energy but no nutritional benefit, like those from sugary drinks and many processed snack foods. And children are simply not getting enough exercise.

I have three of my own, who are now ten, seven and five. Since they were tiny, I have fed them the same foods that my husband and I eat, but it is important to be aware that children under five years old need more fat than older children and adults. Also remember that although it's great to encourage kids to eat plenty of fruit and vegetables, don't allow the very young ones to fill up on too much fibre because they need to leave room for healthy fats and protein to provide the adequate calories and nutrients that they need for growth. Once a child is past the age of five, encourage as much fruit and vegetables as you can.

Children get hungry very quickly, so try to keep healthy snacks available all of the time. In the refrigerator, we always have a bowl of baby carrots, sugarsnap peas, red (bell) peppers, cherry tomatoes and cucumber, which we can all dip into if starving. Wholemeal (whole-wheat) pitta bread and low-fat hummus is a favourite after-school snack. A bowl of olives or cashew nuts on the table keep little tummies happy while I prepare a meal.

My children, like all children, love sweet things and we have the 'sweetie box' on top of the refrigerator, just like I had when I was a little girl. If anyone just has to have a bit of chocolate, it's never refused … I understand that craving so well! However, I buy only the mini chocolate bars and the kids know that they are not allowed to have one until after their meal. They, too, have learned to listen to what their bodies need, and they know that chocolate is a special treat rather than an everyday indulgence.

beef stew with guinness

*everyday**

This guilt-free stew is nutritious and tastes great! Always buy lean meat and cut away any visible fat. If you have recently had a meal containing red meat, use pieces of turkey or chicken instead. The red and green peppers will provide you with vitamins, A, B, C, E plus folate and fibre.

1 Preheat the oven to 150°C/300°F/Gas mark 2.

2 Cut the meat into 3–4cm/1¼–1½in cubes, trimming off any excess fat. Put the flour and black pepper in a bowl and add the cubed meat. Make sure the meat is well dusted with the seasoned flour.

3 In a large frying pan, heat the olive oil over a medium heat and add the meat. Brown on all sides. You may need to do this in two batches. Once browned, put the steak and the remaining flour into a large the casserole dish with a lid. (I use a 4 litre/3½ quart casserole.)

4 Add the bacon and shallots to the frying pan and brown off for about 5 minutes, then add to the casserole. Now add the chopped peppers, ground black pepper and bouquet garni to the casserole.

5 Return the frying pan to the heat and add the Guinness (the alcohol will burn off), tomato purée (paste), sugar and Worcestershire sauce. Bring to the boil, then pour over other the ingredients in the casserole. Add enough stock to cover the meat, and a little bit more!

6 Cook in the oven, with the lid on, for about 3 hours, stirring occasionally, until the meat is tender. Serve hot with mashed potato (see page 100).

*try to limit eating red meat to once or twice a week

serves 4

1kg/2lb 4oz best-quality, super lean stewing steak

1 tbsp plain (all-purpose) flour

freshly ground black pepper

3 tbsp olive oil

6 rashers (slices) very lean back bacon (Canadian bacon), cut into cubes

10–12 shallots, peeled and halved

1 red and 1 green (bell) pepper, deseeded and chopped

1 bouquet garni

350ml/12fl oz/1½ cups Guinness (optional; you can replace this with stock)

3 tbsp tomato purée (paste)

½ tbsp sugar

slurp of Worcestershire sauce

300ml/10fl oz/1¼ cups beef or vegetable stock

salt

Salt can be a silent killer! If you eat too much, it causes high blood pressure, which can lead to strokes and heart attacks. The problem these days is that large quantities of salt are hidden in everyday processed foods. But as long as you don't eat too much processed food, it's OK to add a little salt to your cooking every now and again. I have used celery salt in a few of my recipes in this book, and that's fine for me because I don't eat any processed food.

If you are struggling because you miss having salt with your food, be sure to have some quarters of lemon on the table and just squeeze them over your food. Lemon will give you the same 'bite' as salt but without the hidden dangers. Or, make my Black Pepper and Garlic Crush – a great little trick for adding an intense flavour to your food: Make sure you have a good-sized pestle and mortar. Add peeled garlic cloves and whole black peppercorns and crush together. You may then add lemon or lime juice. Herbs add another dimension; rosemary is my favourite. Just crush it all together and use this as a dry marinade for meat or fish.

lamb rogan josh

everyday*

Chunks of tender lamb flavoured with cinnamon, cardamom and cloves and cooked with only a dash of olive oil make this a healthy alternative to the popular restaurant choice.

1 Remove all visible fat from the lamb steaks and cut into pieces 2.5cm/1in square.

2 In a large frying pan, over a medium heat, warm the olive oil and add the onion, garlic and red (bell) pepper and fry for 4-5 minutes, or until starting to soften.

3 Next, add all the powdered spices and fry for 1 minute. (Add a little water if it becomes too dry.)

4 Add the lamb, tomatoes, bay leaf, pieces of cinnamon, cardamoms, cloves, sugar and stock and simmer over a medium-low heat until reduced and thickened.

5 Chop the coriander (cilantro) and stir in. Serve with freshly steamed vegetables.

* try to limit eating red meat to once or twice a week

serves 4

450g/1lb lamb steaks

2 tbsp olive oil

1 onion, peeled and finely chopped

3 garlic cloves, peeled and finely chopped

1 red (bell) pepper, deseeded and finely chopped

1 tsp ground coriander

1 tsp paprika

1 tsp ground ginger

1 tsp chilli powder

400g/14oz can chopped tomatoes

1 bay leaf

2 x 2cm/¾in pieces of cinnamon stick

4 cardamom pods

3 cloves

1 tsp sugar

200ml/7fl oz/generous ¾ cup chicken stock

small handful of fresh coriander (cilantro)

portion sizes

We are incredibly lucky in the Western world that not many of us have to go hungry. I don't think that my children have ever felt hungry for more than 30 minutes. Hunger is not a pleasant or positive feeling for most of us.

Keeping this thought in mind, consider the portion sizes of your meals. How do you feel after you have eaten? Do you feel 'stuffed' and unable to move or do you feel energetic and light?

A healthy portion size is difficult to quantify, so it's best that you listen to what your body is telling you. If you are overweight and would like to slim down, one of the first things to do is use a smaller plate ... and don't pile it too high. Yes, I am serious! I serve an adult meal on a nine-inch plate and find this is perfectly adequate. Of course, it does matter what kind of food you fill your plate with, but if you stick to the principles of the recipes in this book, you'll be doing fine.

I know we all have days when, as my granny used to say, you can't find your 'fill'. I have days when I am absolutely famished. It usually happens at a certain time of the month or after a particularly busy and energetic period, and at these times my portion sizes increase. But I always feel better if I finish before I am 'stuffed' and I still feel able to get up and get busy. If you are used to eating bigger portions, cut down bit by bit and make sure that vegetables make up the largest proportion of your meal.

Your body can sometimes confuse hunger with thirst, so the next time you think you're hungry try drinking a glass of water before you reach for the snacks or tuck into a big meal.

As a guide, try to limit your bread, pasta, potato or rice to a portion about the size of your closed fist. The same goes for meat, chicken and fish, but double the quantity for vegetables or fruits.

Remember that restaurants usually serve portions that are double the size of a normal healthy meal portion. If you need to eat out regularly for work, don't be afraid to ask for a half-sized portion!

speedy, healthy sausages and beans

*everyday**

You can spice up this recipe as much as you like (or not), but this is a great dish for a crowd. You can very easily increase the amounts to feed many hungry mouths, yet it's so quick, easy and healthy too!

1 Cut each of the sausages into four.

2 In a large, lidded frying pan, heat the oil over a high heat. Add the chopped sausages and sizzle away for 7 minutes, or until they are browned on all sides.

3 Then add the onion, carrots, celery and peas or French beans. Cook for another 5 minutes, or until the onions are beginning to soften.

4 Next, add the canned beans, vegetable or chicken stock and Worcestershire sauce. Bring to the boil, then cover and cook for about 15 minutes, or until the carrots are tender.

5 Finally, stir in the mustard, chopped parsley and season to taste with black pepper if required.

6 Serve steaming hot with lots of chunky wholemeal (whole-wheat) bread to mop up the yummy sauce!

*as long as you use best-quality, low-fat sausages. When buying sausages, shop around for ones that are very low in fat and salt, and have a high meat content (at least 85 per cent).

serves 4, or increase the quantities to serve more

8 best-quality sausages (see note below)

1 tbsp olive oil

1 onion, peeled and chopped

3 carrots, sliced chunkily

4 celery sticks, sliced

handful of French beans, peas or mangetout (snow peas)

2 x 400g/14oz cans mixed beans (kidney, haricot, etc.), drained and rinsed

400ml/14fl oz/1¾ cups chicken or vegetable stock

slurp of Worcestershire sauce

2 tbsp Dijon mustard

handful chopped fresh parsley

freshly ground black pepper

paprika pork with fennel and caraway

everyday

This is a lovely easy dish and makes a nice change from chicken! Very tasty, low in fat, no salt, and when served with pasta or brown rice and steamed green vegetables, it provides a filling nutritious meal that will keep you topped up for hours!

serves 4

1 tbsp olive oil

4 boneless pork steaks

1 large onion, peeled and thinly sliced

400g/14oz can chopped tomatoes

1 garlic clove, peeled and crushed

1 tsp fennel seeds, lightly crushed

½ tsp caraway seeds, crushed

good sprinkling of fresh rosemary

1 tbsp paprika, plus extra to garnish

freshly ground black pepper

2 tbsp soured cream or low-fat crème fraîche

1 Heat the oil in a large frying pan over a fairly high heat. Add the pork steaks and brown quickly on both sides. Lift out the steaks and put them on a plate.

2 Add the onion to the oil remaining in the pan, turning down to a medium heat. Cook for 10 minutes, or until soft and golden. Stir in the tomatoes, garlic, fennel and caraway seeds, rosemary and paprika.

3 Return the pork to the pan and simmer gently for 20-30 minutes, or until tender. Season with plenty of black pepper. Lightly swirl in the soured cream or crème fraîche and sprinkle with a little extra paprika. Serve with brown rice or pasta and sliced steamed courgettes (zucchini) or other green steamed vegetables.

sausages and mash

everyday*

Who doesn't love bangers and mash? When cooked in the right way, this comforting dish can be eaten with no guilt attached.

serves 4

450g/1lb Russet (baking) potatoes or any white mashing potato

450g/1lb sweet potatoes

12 best-quality sausages (3 each is plenty!)

175–250ml/6–8fl oz/³/₄–1 cup semi-skimmed (low-fat) milk

freshly ground black pepper

1 tsp wholegrain mustard

handful of fresh chives, chopped

for the gravy:

1 tbsp olive oil

1 medium onion, peeled and finely sliced

1 garlic clove, peeled and crushed (optional)

2 heaped tbsp shop-bought (store-bought) gravy granules

700ml/1¼ pints/3 cups boiling water (if possible, use the potato cooking water)

1 Preheat the oven to 180°C/350°F/Gas mark 4.

2 Peel all the potatoes and cut into 5cm/2in pieces.

3 Place the sausages in the oven on a wire rack inside a baking tray. (That way, if any fat does come out of the sausages, they will not re-absorb it).

4 Meanwhile, in a large heavy saucepan, simmer the potatoes in boiling water for 20–25 minutes. At the same time, put the olive oil, onions and garlic into a medium-sized pan. Over a low-medium heat, sauté to soften, stirring regularly. (The sausages will take about 35 minutes to cook, so you will have plenty of time to get everything else ready.)

5 After 20–25 minutes, check that the potatoes are nice and tender. Drain the water through a colander into a jug (pitcher) containing the gravy granules.

6 Mix the gravy and add to the saucepan with the onions and garlic. Stir well and just allow to simmer on a very low heat.

7 Meanwhile, return the potatoes to the large saucepan and add the milk. With a potato masher or hand blender, mash the potatoes until smooth, adding more milk, if necessary, to make creamy.

8 Serve the sausages on a bed of mash potato with the delicious onion gravy poured over the top.

* as long as you use best-quality, low-fat sausages

cut back on the alcohol

I'm sure you've heard about the benefits of a 'Mediterranean Diet'. The Mediterranean diet is especially high in antioxidants, found in the fresh fruits, vegetables and olive oil eaten by people living around the Mediterranean. (Extra-virgin olive oil is one of the few oils that require no chemical processing and so it retains the natural flavours, vitamins, minerals, antioxidants and other healthy constituents of the ripe olive fruit.) Followers of the diet also enjoy a glass or two of red wine with their meal, which is also proven to be beneficial in guarding against heart disease. So, there is research that will support moderate alcohol consumption in a healthy diet. However, it's important to follow guidelines for sensible drinking because too much alcohol can seriously damage your health and put stress on your heart.

As a general guide:
- Men should consume no more than three to four units per day with at least two alcohol-free days per week
- Women should consume no more than two to three units per day with at least two alcohol free days per week
- 1 unit of alcohol = 300ml/½ pint of ordinary-strength beer, lager or cider;
  a small glass (125ml/4fl oz) of wine;
  a single measure of spirit or a small glass (50ml/2fl oz) of fortified wine such as sherry or port.

You'll see throughout my recipes that I offer an alternative to alcohol if you prefer to not to use it. However, please note that most of the alcohol burns off in the cooking process.

desserts

a note on desserts

I'm often asked if I have any recipes for 'healthy' desserts and I usually struggle with this. Apart from the obvious – fresh fruit salad and possibly yogurt – puddings are generally loaded with butter, cream and/or sugar, so it's difficult to come up with something that is both healthy and tasty.

However, I do have a philosophy on this subject, which I feel sure you're going to like.

Life is short and puddings are delicious! Therefore, once you have cut out all the junk and all the processed food and you are confident that you are giving yourself and your family the best health benefits through the great food that you eat, you deserve a treat. And if there is a scrumptious, delicious, gorgeous pudding that is winking seductively at you, begging to be tasted, then go for it! Just not every day and not with every meal!

baked bananas with apricots
everyday*

The most simple ideas often create the most delicious flavours! This is a favourite with the children served with ice-cream, but I love it served on its own as a nutritious energy provider that takes just a minute to prepare.

1 Preheat the oven to 190°C/375°F/Gas mark 4.

2 Cut 4 rectangles of foil, 30 x 25cm/12 x 10in each.

3 Peel the bananas and cut in half lengthways. Put 2 banana halves in the centre of each foil rectangle and put to one side.

4 Drain the apricots and tip into a food processor with the honey. Whiz for just a few seconds until you have a smooth fruit purée.

5 Spoon the purée over the bananas and fold the foil over to create airtight parcels (pockets). Put these onto a baking tray to catch any leaking juices and bake in the oven for 10 minutes.

6 Open the parcels and transfer the banana and apricot mixture onto plates, then sprinkle with the flaked (slivered) almonds. Serve with crème fraîche, probiotic low-fat yogurt or ice-cream if you like, but this is delicious without! (My children also like to add a dusting of cocoa powder/unsweetened cocoa.)

* served without the ice-cream

serves 4

4 bananas

400g/14oz can halved apricots in juice

1 tbsp honey

4 tbsp flaked (slivered) almonds

small scoop of low-fat crème fraîche, probiotic yogurt or ice-cream, to serve (optional)

bbq fruit skewers

everyday*

Serve without the ice-cream for an everyday treat, but I'd save it for a treat and go for ice-cream with this dish every time! You'll need a hot barbecue for this, or you can grill (broil) on a very high heat.

serves 4

1 or 2 skewers each, depending on how much fruit you add

75g/3oz/generous ⅓ cup Muscavado sugar

1 tsp ground cinnamon

pinch of freshly grated nutmeg

125ml/4fl oz/½ cup orange juice

20–30 chunks or slices of ripe tropical fruits, such as strawberries, papayas, bananas, mangoes and pineapple

fresh mint sprigs, to garnish (optional)

a small scoop of crème fraîche, probiotic low-fat yogurt or ice-cream, to serve (optional)

wooden skewers, soaked in water to cover for 1 hour, then drained

1 Combine the sugar, cinnamon and nutmeg in a small bowl.

2 Skewer the fruit on the wooden skewers, alternating fruits and placing 3-5 pieces on each.

3 Dip each kebab in the orange juice, then sprinkle with the spiced sugar.

4 Arrange the skewers on the hot barbecue and cook until nicely browned on both sides, 3-4 minutes per side.

5 Garnish with mint leaves, (if using) and serve immediately.

* when served without the ice-cream, and feel free to omit the sugar

spicy poached pears

treat

A very elegant and sophisticated dish. Feel free to swap the red wine for red grape juice, although most of the alcohol does burn off during cooking (and makes the recipe extra-specially delicious!).

serves 4

8 firm pears

1 vanilla pod (bean)

1 cinnamon stick

1 large glass red wine (300ml/10fl oz/1¼ cups)

300ml/10fl oz/1¼ cups water

175g/6oz/generous ¾ cup sugar (granulated or caster/superfine)

low-fat crème fraîche or probiotic yogurt, to serve

1 Preheat the oven to 150º/300ºF/Gas mark 2.

2 Peel the whole pears, keeping the stalks attached. Arrange them in a deep ovenproof dish large enough to take all eight pears without too much room to spare, then add the scraped vanilla pod and seeds and the stick of cinnamon.

3 Mix together the red wine and water, and pour over the pears to almost cover them.

4 Cook in the oven for about 2 hours, turning over occasionally.

5 When the pears are lovely and soft, take them out of the oven and remove from the liquid.

6 Remove the spices and pour the remaining liquid into a small saucepan. Simmer over a medium heat until the liquid turns thick and syrupy, then pour over the pears to serve.

7 Serve either warm or cold with crème fraîche or yogurt.

red berry meringue pie

treat

This pie calls for no pastry, so while it still contains a bit of sugar it has virtually no fat. It's also easy to make and tastes absolutely delicious. I have a really sweet tooth, and I like the way the slightly sharp taste of the fruit is cut by the sweet meringue. The almonds add extra crunch and texture, and the fat they contain is a healthy fat.

1 Preheat the oven to 200°C/400°F/Gas mark 6.

2 Divide the almonds between the four ramekins and place on the bottom.

3 Wash and prepare the fruit, hulling the strawberries but leaving them whole. Then mix the berries together and put on top of the almonds. Make sure you fill the ramekins to only halfway.

4 Preferably with an electric whisk, whisk the egg whites in a clean bowl until they form stiff peaks

5 Add half the sugar and whisk again until the mixture 'shines'.

6 Fold in the remaining sugar and divide the meringue between the four dishes.

7 Bake in the oven for 15 minutes. Then remove and leave to cool for about 5 minutes before serving. Be careful, because the fruit will be extremely hot!

serves 4

115g/4oz whole, unblanced almonds (optional)

175g/6oz/1½ cups strawberries

175g/6oz/1½ cups raspberries

175g/6oz/1½ cups blueberries

3 egg whites

175 g/6oz/generous ¾ cup caster sugar

4 x 9cm/3½in diameter ramekins

Omit the almonds if you are serving anyone with a nut allergy. Otherwise, try sprinkling a few crushed almonds on top of the meringue before cooking – delicious!

crunchy rhubarb crumble

treat

This dish is extra scrummy and has a 'sticky toffee pudding' vibe going on due to the dates and honey. Unlike traditional crumble it doesn't contain butter or a lot of sugar. The rhubarb contains plenty of vitamin C and is a good source of potassium, and the wholemeal breadcrumbs and porridge oats offer good dietary roughage. Easy as pie to make, and a crowd-pleaser every time!

serves 4

1lb/450g rhubarb, washed, trimmed and cut into 2cm/³/4 in chunks

grated rind and juice of 1 orange

50g/1³/4oz pitted dates, chopped

3 tbsp clear honey

75g/3oz wholemeal (whole-wheat) breadcrumbs

75g/3oz rolled porridge oats (oatmeal)

75g/3oz polyunsaturated margarine, melted

50g/1³/4oz demerara (turbinado) sugar

1 Preheat the oven to 180°C/350°F/Gas mark 4.

2 Put the chopped rhubarb, orange juice and rind, dates and honey in a 1 litre/4 cup ovenproof dish.

3 Mix all the other ingredients together in a large bowl and spread over the fruit.

4 Bake for about 35 minutes, or until gorgeously golden, then serve immediately with low-fat custard, ice-cream or a big dollop of crème fraîche.

When buying margarine for cooking, always go for a product that is high in polyunsaturated fat (which contains good omega-3 and -6 fatty acids) rather than saturated fat. Avoid those containing hydrogenated fat.

when is a treat not a treat?

This is easy to answer: a treat is not a treat when it happens more than twice a week. There you go; it even rhymes, which means it is even easier to remember!

I sometimes feel I am a split personality. On the one hand, I am someone with a serious heart condition, who must take things easy and look after myself. On the other hand, I am someone who knows only too well that life is short and I have a burning desire to live life to the full and not miss out on *anything*!

So, when celebrating a precious friend's birthday or a meal out with friends or just a night in front of a long-awaited movie with the children, a treat should be anticipated and enjoyed with guilt-free abandon! We love puddings in our house – but not every day!

If you struggle because of a very sweet tooth, try to go for fruit-based desserts with just a little ice-cream or low-fat probiotic yogurt. You can probably satisfy your craving without going overboard on the portion sizes.

I had a friend who used to keep just two squares of dark chocolate in her handbag at a time. Then when she got the urge for something sweet, she had a little something special on hand that would satisfy her but not blow her healthy eating out of the water.

I think it's always better to have a little something of what you fancy instead of denying yourself for too long and then going crazy and devouring a whole chocolate cake and regretting it for the rest of the week!

tarik's apple puff squares
treat

My son, Tarik, invented this dish and he loves to make it himself. I used to help him slice the apples nice and thin, but he soon mastered the skill. Here I show you how to make individual Apple Puff Squares, but you can just as easily make one large one!

The light puff pastry is a great alternative to shortcrust, making this a healthier alternative to apple pie.

makes about 12 squares

500g/1lb 2oz ready-made puff pastry, rolled out into 2 sheets 30 x 30cm/12 x 12in

3 granny smith apples, cored and finely sliced

2 tbsp demerara (turbinado) sugar, plus 1 tbsp for sprinkling

1½ tsp ground cinnamon

pinch of freshly grated nutmeg

lemon zest or orange zest

1 beaten egg, for brushing the pastry

1. Preheat the oven to 200°C/400°F/Gas mark 6.

2. Spread out the puff pastry and cut into 12 x 10cm/ 4½ x 4in squares (approximately) and place on a lined baking sheet.

3. Core and slice the apples as finely as you can.

4. Toss the apples in the sugar, cinnamon, nutmeg and zest.

5. Arrange 4-5 apple slices on each pastry square, leaving a border of pastry around the outside. It's OK to overlap the apples slightly, but you don't want the apples to be too thick or heavy - this is a very light dish.

6. Brush the outside edge of the pastry with the beaten egg and sprinkle all over with sugar.

7. Bake in the oven for about 20 minutes.

orange and peach filo parcels
treat

These low-fat parcels (pockets) are like golden presents wrapped in brown paper. It's only when you open them up and taste the insides that you appreciate the flavour and aroma of the cooked fruit and sweet maple syrup.

makes 6 parcels

3 oranges

3 peaches or nectarines

2 tbsp maple syrup

50ml/2fl oz/¼ cup water

1 tbsp light olive oil

12 sheets filo (phyllo) pastry, each cut into 18cm/7in squares

icing (confectioners') sugar, to dust

6 x 9cm/3½in diameter ramekin dishes

1 Preheat the oven to 200°C/400°F/Gas mark 6.

2 Using a small knife, remove the peel and pith from the oranges and cut in between each segment.

3 Wash and slice up the peaches or nectarines into similar sized pieces as the orange segments.

4 Put the fruit, maple syrup and water into a large pan and simmer over a medium heat for 3 minutes. Take off the heat and strain over a jug (pitcher), saving the juices for later. Lightly oil the ramekins.

5 Brush one of the filo (phyllo) squares with a little oil, then lay another square on top and brush again. Turn over so that the greased side is facing down, then gently push the double filo square into a ramekin.

6 Repeat with the remaining pastry to line the remaining ramekins.

7 Divide the fruit among the ramekins. Gather up the filo edges and twist together lightly to seal. Transfer ramekins to a non-stick baking sheet and bake for 25–30 minutes, or until crisp and golden.

8 While your parcels are cooking, pour the juices into a small saucepan and simmer until reduced by half.

9 When the parcels are cooked, remove from the ramekins and put onto plates. Dust with icing (confectioners') sugar and serve with the reduced juice poured over. Yummy!

frozen yogurt tubs

everyday*

My children love these as much as ice-cream. And I love them because I know I'm adding vitamins and antioxidants to their diets with every delicious mouthful without giving them the unnecessary fats – and all that fruit is packed with goodness too!

Out of season, replace the berries with the same quantity of frozen forest fruits, such as redcurrants and blackcurrants.

1 Simply place all the ingredients in a food processor and whiz up until nicely blended.

2 Spoon into six small plastic tubs (each about 8cm/3¼in diameter) and pop into the freezer for at least 4 hours.

serves 6

500g/1lb 2oz tub natural low-fat yogurt

4 tbsp icing (confectioners') sugar, or to taste

500g/1lb 2oz your choice of summer fruits (strawberries, raspberries, blackberries, blueberries)

* if served in a small portion. Although this dish contains sugar, the nutrients from the fruit far outweigh the negatives.

wholemeal banana bread with poppy seeds

everyday*

Instead of cake, reach for this lovely, moist, high-fibre loaf. It's great straight out of the oven, cold or even toasted. The fibre will keep the hunger pangs at bay and keep you feeling full up for longer. It has a lower fat and sugar content than regular cake and since even a small slice is very filling, you can keep your portion sizes down too. This recipe is good for using up overripe bananas, so it's also great for cutting down on waste!

I find a 20 x 10cm (8 x 4in) loaf tin works best for this recipe. Mine is non-stick, but this is quite a sticky loaf, so it's always a good idea to line the base with baking (parchment) paper.

1. Preheat the oven to 160°C/325°F/Gas mark 3.

2. Put the sugar, egg, fromage frais and oil in a large bowl and whisk together well.

3. Slowly stir in the bananas and sultanas (golden raisins).

4. Next add the flour, bicarbonate of soda (baking soda), poppy seeds, cinnamon and nutmeg and fold gently with a metal spoon.

5. Spoon the mixture into your prepared loaf tin and bake for about 50 minutes.

6. Test the bread with a skewer after this time. Push the skewer into the centre of the loaf – if it comes out clean, the bread is cooked; if it's still wet, it needs about another 5 minutes.

* if served in a small portion. A larger piece would be a treat!

serves 1 loaf cake

100g/3½oz/½ cup (solidly packed) dark muscovado

1 egg

200g/7oz/generous ¾ cup low-fat fromage frais or yogurt

2 tbsp light olive oil

2 ripe bananas, mashed

40g/1½oz/scant ⅓ cup sultanas (golden raisins)

150g/5½ oz/1 cup wholemeal (whole-wheat) self-raising (self-rising) flour

½ tsp bicarbonate of soda (baking soda)

3 tbsp poppy seeds

1 tsp ground cinnamon

1 tsp ground nutmeg

tuscan grape cake

treat

This is an extra-special indulgence, perfect for a birthday celebration. It's by no means an everyday dish, but as celebrations and a good cake go hand in hand, I would never deprive myself, or you! You'll see that it contains sugar and butter, which are ingredients that I usually avoid in my day-to-day diet, however, life's too short never to have a special treat, and I'd rather have a small slice of this delicious delight than a shop-bought cake. The wine in this recipe gets cooked away. This cake will make 16–18 slices.

makes 1 x 23cm/9in round cake

225ml/8fl oz/1 cup sweet white wine

175ml/6fl oz/¾ cup extra-virgin olive oil

225g/8oz plain (all-purpose) flour, plus 1 tbsp for dusting

200g/7oz/1 cup light muscovado sugar

115g/4oz/1 stick butter, softened

3 eggs

zest of 1 orange and 1 lemon

1 tsp baking powder

175g/6oz/generous 1 cup grapes, halved and deseeded

4–5 tbsp demerara (turbinado) sugar

1 Preheat the oven to 180°C/350°F/Gas mark 4.

2 Pour the wine into a saucepan. Bring to the boil, then simmer until reduced down to about 6 tablespoons; this will take 5–10 minutes. Leave to cool.

3 Brush a 23cm/9in spring-form cake tin with olive oil, tip in 1 tablespoon flour, then shake all over the pan until covered. Discard any excess.

4 Beat together the sugar and butter until creamy. Add the eggs, one at a time, then stir in the zests.

5 Stir together the cooled wine and olive oil, then pour a little into the cake mix. Stir, then fold in a third of the flour and all the baking powder. Keep alternating between adding the remaining liquid and flour until everything has been incorporated and the batter is smooth.

6 Spoon the cake batter into the prepared tin, then smooth the surface with the back of the spoon.

7 Scatter the halved grapes, cut side down, over the top, then sprinkle over the demerara sugar.

8 Bake for 35–40 minutes, or until a skewer inserted into the middle of the cake comes out clean. Eat warm or cool. This will store in an airtight container for up to 3 days.

calories are great!

Really! The right kind of calories *are* great! Without calories, we would die. When we take in calories, they are turned into fuel or energy that enables us to move, to exercise, even to think.

You'll notice that I don't show the calorie content in my recipes. That is because I don't believe in counting calories on the way in; I believe in concentrating more on the calories that get burned off by exercise, because exercise is what helps enormously to give me my good health. I'm not advocating a high-calorie diet, far from it, but as long as my food is prepared without excessive fat, sugar or salt, I know the calorie content is reasonable and beneficial to me. It's that easy.

Recently I watched in horror as a TV show slammed the merits of the fruit smoothie, claiming that they shouldn't be allowed because they contain more calories than a can of Coke! Well, I jumped around my living room getting into a right ol' stew because the TV chef who passed on this useless piece of information was completely missing the point.

Healthy eating isn't just about calories. Healthy eating is about nourishment. Certainly, it's true that it is important to avoid too many 'empty' calories', which offer no nutritional benefit at all. From unhealthy fats and refined foods, they are completely without benefit to the body and should be avoided. However, 'good' calories from nourishing, vitamin-enriched foods are brilliant and wonderful and should be celebrated – not feared!

Remember that different foods work for you in different ways. You could compare a can of diet drink containing one calorie with an avocado containing maybe 200 calories. Which would you prefer to have for lunch? Sure, the avocado has more calories, but it is full of nourishment, and will keep your energy up throughout the day and help you burn more of the healthy calories you've eaten!

So, go for that smoothie for breakfast or mid-morning snack or whenever you fancy because you will be nourishing your body and giving your energy levels a wonderful boost that in turn will give you fabulous future health. The one-calorie diet drink is a false economy. Your body will still be hungry for nourishment, and you may find yourself reaching for an unhealthy snack loaded with unhealthy calories if you're not careful. So, rather than thinking 'calories', think 'nourishment'. Your body will be happier for longer and the rewards will pay dividends.

drinks

Many people make the mistake of believing that drinking fizzy sweet drinks, such as lemonade or cola, will give them the much needed energy boost they are seeking. Well, they will give you a boost for about five minutes and then your sugar levels will drop dramatically and make you feel more tired than you were in the beginning! Instead, try my delicious and very easy smoothies and Elderflower Fizz. They are much better for you, contain considerably less sugar and will make you feel better in an instant.

elderflower fizz

everyday

Pop 1 small slurp of elderflower cordial (found in supermarkets and health-food stores) in a large glass. Add some sparkling mineral water, a squeeze of fresh lime and some ice cubes, and enjoy.

green goodness smoothie

everyday

Take 115g/4oz/1 cup green seedless grapes, 2 kiwi fruits, 5cm/2in piece of cucumber, 1 sweet apple, 250ml/8fl oz/1 cup mango juice and 5 ice cubes and whiz them together in a blender. Serve immediately.

ruby red smoothie

everyday

Take 115g/4oz/1 cup strawberries, 115g/4oz/1 cup raspberries, 125ml/4fl oz/1/2 cup pineapple juice, 250ml/8fl oz/1 cup low-fat natural yogurt and 5 ice cubes and whiz them together in a blender. Serve immediately.

Tip: You can use frozen berries in place of the ice cubes.

epilogue: the proof of the pudding is in the eating

I wrote the introduction to the original publication of this book almost four years ago. When I look back I see that, although I thought I had recovered very well from my heart attacks, I was actually only at the very beginning of my journey. I suppose, in truth, this journey of mine will continue until the very end of my life.

I often surprise people by saying that I'm not sorry that I suffered heart attacks when I did. This may be a difficult concept to understand, but I believe that many people who have been in a similar situation to me might understand what I mean. Of course, I wish I didn't have the ongoing health problems, but I honestly can't say that my life is any worse now because of what happened to me. And in fact I would go as far as to say that it is much richer, fuller, more meaningful and certainly much more fun because of what I have learned from what happened to me. I believe I know what is important, I no longer waste my time on negative things, feelings or thoughts, and I hope I am able to help many, many people have a greater quality of life and a better, healthier future.

Initially, after my heart attacks, I was afraid of everything. Afraid to sneeze, laugh, cry, get angry, afraid to get excited, afraid to feel any emotion at all. These were very difficult hurdles to overcome. I nearly died, and although I survived, no doctor was able to tell me that it wouldn't happen again or that my heart wouldn't just stop working because of the amount of damage I had suffered. Getting to the point where I had to decide to stop surviving and start living again was even more frightening than the attacks themselves. But I knew I had to do it.

I had three young children who looked to me for everything and I had to find a way to put my fears aside and be a great mum again!

A major part of this process was doing everything possible to give myself the best chance of recovery. I realized very early on that the food I ate had a significant effect on my body. If I ate food with chemicals, preservatives and colourings, I very quickly began to feel unwell. One particular Indian take-away landed me straight back in hospital, so strong was the effect. The MSG (monosodium glutamate) in the meal caused my heart to enter a dangerous pattern that went way beyond a palpitation attack. When someone with a 'healthy' heart eats a meal like this, they also will be affected, but probably won't notice. I guess my body is like touch paper for food trials. If anyone is going to react, I will. But that's not to say it isn't happening to you, too. You just don't feel it ... yet.

Five years on from my heart attacks, I am strong, fit and funky! My cardiologists continue to be impressed with my progress and still find it hard to explain why I show no residual symptoms of my heart failure. I can explain. I can feel why I am doing so well. Every time I eat a nourishing meal, it helps give me the energy to live my (very busy) life. I have the energy to do a little bit of exercise, walk the dog, chase the kids – or my husband if I feel so inclined! And if I slip, for just one meal, I suffer. My energy levels drop, I feel tired and I struggle with my day. It is that simple and straightforward.

I hope that you have energy to live your life to the full and if you struggle sometimes, try eating for nourishment as I do. Not only will you get some bounce in your step but it might just save your life.

Index